THE QUAKER SERGEANT'S WAR

~THE~
QUAKER
SERGEANT'S
WAR

The Civil War Diary
of
Sergeant David M. Haworth
Third Tennessee Infantry USA

EDITED

BY

GENE ALLEN

Fort Worth, Texas

TCU Box 298300
Fort Worth, Texas 76129
817.257.7822
www.prs.tcu.edu
To order books: 1.800.826.8911

Design by David Timmons

Cover illustration: *A regiment waiting for the order to march*, courtesy of the Library of
Congress

Dedicated to the members of the Haworth family
past and present
In appreciation of their efforts in building and preserving
the Union we now enjoy

CONTENTS

2

1862

I was ordered to come to New market to Drill
But didnt go so fry sent 10 men of his Co
out to get me but I never they was comeing
And I went across the river and Staid on till
they went back after that I kept hid out
on till the 8th day of april 1862 Just about
Sun down 3 of us boys My oldest Brother
William C Haworth Isaac B and my self left
home bid our Mother & father good by and Started
for Kentucky for the purpos of joining the union
Army oald Ruben first across halstein river at
Stones ferry in a canoe Near John Sawyears A gide
took harge of us we travelid that night through
the woddes in single file no one to speak above
A whifper wadeing Creekes and reached the widdow
Sawyers farm Just before day we lay hid in and old
horse at the back side of her farm it was filed with
fodder and when night come we was called out
And give Instructions by Sawyear then Started on
our Journey four the promas land

PREFACE

The diary entries that appear in this book were actually transcribed by hand from the diary David Haworth carried during the conflict. David Haworth himself transcribed his entries. It can only be surmised that the original suffered considerable damage on the battlefield, since the equipment they carried and the soldiers themselves were exposed to the elements—rain, snow, mud—even theirs and their comrades' lifeblood—for four years. At the top of each page of his transcript, David wrote the year the events transpired, often adding the month at the beginning of the first line on the page. Since these often interrupt a sentence begun on the preceding page, they have been omitted or moved, with editor's replacements appearing in brackets. In many instances bracketed dates have been added by the editor for the reader's convenience. Dates are also included in David's entries as he wrote them.

Current scholarly practice dictates that historical documents be transcribed as they were written, regardless of irregularities in spelling, capitalization, punctuation, or grammar. TCU Press has followed this practice in this volume. David's spelling was left intact; an occasional gloss in brackets following a misspelled word appears where it may help comprehension. Words David inserted above the line are indicated by carats (^ ^). David Haworth's spelling variations and usage are quite typical of nineteenth-century writers. In contrast to the Haworth transcript, however, other contemporary accounts presented in this book—letters, announcements, journals, and so forth—were drawn from previously published accounts that almost certainly were edited for grammar, spelling, capitalization, and punctuation by their publishers.

ACKNOWLEDGMENTS

One person may be listed as "author," or in this case "editor," but anyone who has been through this process knows there are many, many others who bring a book to completion. In this case, Robert Wright's early interest and support was crucial. It was David Swan Haworth's foresight that preserved David Haworth's diary when it might well have been lost forever. Ron Haworth and Marilyn Winton Totten, long-time leaders in the Haworth Family Association, provided invaluable information on the history of the family, and Carol Rodriquez started the whole thing by lending me a copy of David's diary several years ago. Nephew Chris Gray discovered a tintype portrait of David, the only one we have, in the depths of my grandmother's closet (David was her uncle). Daughter Nancy is the most amazing genealogy researcher I know and came up with all manner of documents that contributed greatly to parts of the story initially unknown to the family. Artists Cheryl Allen, James Gray, and James Anderson provided invaluable graphic support. And of course, the invaluable, almost daily assistance of the entire staff at TCU Press.

Every writer's wife will appreciate my wife Cheryl's contribution to this book . . . just the right amount of persistence, praise, and patience. Each at the proper time.

after 4 nightes of Hard marching never travveled in a road Jouss [just] at night on the fifth day we come into London Ky whear the government had a recruiting station thear was the stars and stripes on a big flag pole we marched around that with our hates off cherring for Uncle Sam. . . . The next morning I couldent get my boots on and they was calling for all men that wanted to join the armey to get in line I went out in my sock feet and lined up

INTRODUCTION

David M. Haworth was born September 4, 1842 on a four-hundred-acre farm close by the Holston River in Jefferson County, East Tennessee, four miles west of the little town of New Market. The Haworths had been in the New World for a long time. George Haworth, a weaver from an upland village in Lancashire in the northeast of England, arrived in the summer of 1699 and, after a short stay with his sister in Delaware, went to the Philadelphia area. William Penn arrived in December of that same year. George's experiences in his new home were well documented in letters back to England. He was a member of the Society of Friends, also known as Quakers.

Over the years the Haworths, like much of the rest of the nation, moved west. The Quakers tended to migrate in small family groups, establishing Quaker meetings as they moved. They used the term "meeting" to identify a specific group location. The Haworth migration path generally flowed from Pennsylvania through western Virginia to Tennessee, then northward again into Ohio, Indiana, and Illinois. David's family settled in East Tennessee.

Tennessee was a state with a split personality, both geographical and political. Like much of the rest of the Deep South, the economy of West Tennessee was structured on the plantation model, which was based on the ownership of slaves. East Tennessee was composed of small farms and timber-covered hills, where there was little incentive for owning slaves. People in West Tennessee tended to identify with the Old South, and those in East Tennessee with the Union. The situation was further complicated by the state's geography: All of East Tennessee's means of transportation—rivers and railroads—ran to the south, while their sympathies went to the north. The independence of the hardy mountaineers did not mesh well with the plantation lifestyles of their fellow citizens in the west. Slowly but surely the nation's attitudes hardened over the issue of slavery, and when Tennessee joined the Confederacy, the last state to do so, the stage was set for what would become the tragedy of East Tennessee.

In 1859, when David was seventeen, he went to Georgetown, Illinois, to visit some of his Haworth relatives. The 1860 census shows him working as a "farm hand" for the Bailey family in Georgetown Township. While there he was caught up in Abraham Lincoln's campaign for the presidency and joined a paramilitary political group called the Wide Awakes. This group of young men was created by the Republican Party as a means of injecting enthusiasm into political rallies, keeping order in the crowds, escorting prominent Republican visitors, and generally making as much noise as possible. Each group was organized along military lines with a captain and one or more lieutenants. David's captain was Henderson Cook.

The usual Wide Awake uniform consisted of a cape, a black glazed hat, and a six-foot torch. The estimated cost of all this was about $1.33. The Wide Awakes held parades, practiced military-style marching, and even learned intricate marching maneuvers.

The standard uniform for Wide Awakes. *Courtesy James Gray.*

There was also a social component to the Wide Awakes, offering the young men a chance to mingle with local unmarried young ladies. One newspaper account mentioned an outing to visit another group in Galena, Illinois. The Galena Wide Awakes were no doubt well organized. Their drillmaster was a local store clerk named Ulysses S. Grant.[1]

David stayed in Illinois through the campaign and remembered seeing the new president as he passed through Danville, Illinois, on his way to

Washington. The train arrived at the Great Western Depot in Danville at noon, the day before Lincoln's fifty-second birthday. Danville was not a planned stop. Perhaps Lincoln had insisted on stopping, even though it put the train behind schedule. He had practiced law in Danville from 1841 to 1859 and had many friends in the town. About one thousand of them waited eagerly to see the man who was about to become president of the United States. Lincoln made a brief speech from the back of the train, then the whistle blew, the train began to move, and the citizens watched Lincoln leave for the last time. For David Haworth it was his first and last glimpse of the man who would soon be his commander-in-chief.

When the war started he made his way back home to the family farm. He returned to a difficult situation. Tennessee was bitterly divided between the western and eastern parts of the state, with the eastern section, the Haworth's, definitely pro-Union.

The Quakers were especially suspect because of their refusal to join in the general war hysteria as well as for their historic opposition to slavery.

We do not know how much pressure was put on the Haworth family at this point by their neighbors. Perhaps they could have continued on with their lives and simply sat out the war.

But in April 1862, the Confederate Congress enacted conscription for all white males aged eighteen to thirty-five. This new reality was announced to the population in a long proclamation from Major General Kirby Smith, Confederate commander of East Tennessee:

To the Disaffected People of East Tennessee:

The Major General commanding this department, charged with the enforcement of martial law, believing that many of its citizens have been misled into the commission of treasonable acts through ignorance of their duties and obligations to their State, and that many have actually fled across the mountains and joined our enemies under the persuasion and misguidance of supposed friends but designing enemies, hereby proclaims:

1st. That no person so misled who comes forward, declares his error, and takes the oath to support the Constitution of the State and of the Confederate States shall be molested or punished on account of past acts or words.

2nd. That no person so persuaded and misguided as to leave his home and join the enemy who shall return within thirty days of the date of this proclamation, acknowledge his error, and take an oath to support the Constitution of the State and of the Confederate States shall be molested or punished on account of past acts or words.

After thus announcing his disposition to treat with the utmost clemency those who have been led away from the true path of patriotic duty the major-general commanding furthermore declares his determination henceforth to employ all the elements at his disposal for the protection of the lives and property of the citizens of East Tennessee, whether from the incursions of the enemy or the irregularities of his own troops and for the suppression of all treasonable practices.

E. Kirby Smith,
Maj.-Gen. Cmdg. Department of East Tennessee.[2]

There was some opposition to the East Tennessee conscription, even among officers of the Confederate army.

SIR: The civil condition of East Tennessee is a subject of solicitude with me. Under the pressure of the enforcement of the conscript act several thousand of the young men of East Tennessee fled the territory and entered the ranks of the Federal Army. Large numbers of others, to avoid the conscription, have fled from their homes and are lurking in the mountains, the woods, and the caves. They are chiefly men of families, who desire to avoid all military service in either army and yet wish to remain near their families. Many of these men, rendered desperate by their situation, are infesting the roads, waylaying the conscript officers, and, urged alike by necessity and a spirit of revenge and bitterness, are stealing horses and destroying the cattle, hogs, and products within their reach. Occasionally their depredations extend to the destruction of barns and house and injury to crops within their reach. The civil arm is paralyzed; the bitterness of faction is intense. The enforcement of order by the military arm, however we may seek to restrain its enemies, will often be attended by instances of unnecessary severity, giving room for the charge of persecution. In whatever light we view it the question is surrounded by difficulties that have doubtless attracted oftentimes the attention of the President. After considering the question as fully as my time will permit, I am convinced that the following policy would be the best solution to the difficult problem:

First. To exempt from conscription for a certain period—say six or eight months—such fugitives as within a limited time will return to the cultivation of their fields and will lead a life of quiet and obedience to the laws. The effect of this would be to disperse or weaken the bands which are scattered through the mountains, to cultivate and gather a more abundant crop, and to put an end to the molestation of the highways and the destruction and stealing of animals.

Second. To such as refuse to avail themselves of these privileges a severe policy should be pursued when practicable. They should be considered as alien enemies in armed opposition to the Government, and when captured regarded as prisoners of war and to be exchanged as such. In very flagrant cases a more severe policy might be pursued, but in most cases it would seem needless to try the offenders before a civil court, on account of the difficulty of obtaining two witnesses to the same overt act. To do so would be equivalent to releasing them in our midst, to renew their former course of depredations.

Third. With a view to local defense against such depredations I am encouraging, with some prospect of success, the formation of volunteer companies for local defense, under the act of October 13, 1862. As the people are generally unarmed, their arms having been taken for other purposes by the State authorities, I propose, with your concurrence, issuing to these organizations the squirrel and shot guns now in the arsenal here. In an emergency these companies may add somewhat to the security of the bridge defenses.

I will thank you to lay these views before the War Department. The question is a most delicate one and very difficult of solution; but I think a temporary exemption would gradually bring back these fugitives to the quiet cultivation of their fields—the best service which they can render the Government.

> I am, sir, very respectfully, your obedient servant,
> S. B. BUCKNER, Maj.-Gen., Cmdg. Department.[3]

General Buckner's suggestions were apparently not adopted. Col. William Churchwell, provost marshal, issued another proclamation:

The undersigned, in executing martial law in this department, assures those interested, who have fled to the enemy's lines and who are actually in their army, that he will welcome their return to their homes and their families. They are offered amnesty and protection if they come to lay down their arms and act as loyal citizens within the thirty days given them by Maj.-Gen. E. Kirby Smith to do so.

At the end of that time those failing to return to their homes and accept the amnesty thus offered and provide for and protect their wives and children in East Tennessee will have them sent to their care in Kentucky or beyond the Confederate States lines at their own expense.

All that leave after this date with a knowledge of the above acts their families will be sent immediately after them. The women and children must be taken care of by husbands and fathers either in East Tennessee or in the Lincoln Government.

W.M. CHURCHWELL,
Col. And Provost Marshal.[4]

For the Haworth boys there was no longer any option. And that is where David takes up his remarkable story.

CHAPTER ONE
~ 1862 ~

Henrey Fry was makeing up a company of inft.[infantry] at New market and offered to make me his 1st Liutenent if I would join the Confederate armey. I had had some military training, and t[h]ey wanted me for Drill master but I was for the Union couldent go with the South. I was ordered to come to New market to Drill But didn't go so fry sent 10 men of his Co out to get me but I new they was comeing and I went across the river and staid on ountill they went back. After that I kept hid out ountill the 8th day of April 1862.

Posters like this encouraged the young men of Jefferson County to join the Confederate cause, with just a mention of what would happen if they didn't. *Courtesy Library of Congress, Printed Ephemera Collection, Portfolio 175 Folder 21, http://hdl.loc.gov/loc.rbc/rbpe.17502100.*

THE VOLUNTARY MANNER IN WHICH SOME OF THE SOUTHERN VOLUNTEERS ENLIST.

Cartoon courtesy of the Congressional Library.

[April 8, 1862]
Joust [just] *about sun down 3 of us boyes, my oldest Brother William C. Haworth, Isaac B. and my self left home bid our mother and father good by and started for Kentukey for the purpos of joining the Union Army.*

The youngest Haworth brother, John, was left behind, probably because of his age. He later joined an East Tennessee cavalry unit, however, and eventually transferred into the Third Tennessee Infantry to be with his brothers.

oold Ruben put ^us^ acros Holsten river at Stones Ferry in a cano[e]. Thear John Sawyears a gide took charge of us. We travveled that night through the woddes in single file no one to

*speake above a whi[sp]er wadeing creeks and reached the widdow
Sawyers farm jouus [just] befor day. We lay hid in and old hous at
the back side of her farm it was filled with fodder and when night
come we was called out and giv[en] instructions by Sawyear then
started on our journey f[or] the promas [promised] land. We was
soon joined by other squades ountill before morning we numbered
115. And from there on we was pileted by Lafayet Rutherford
and John Sawyers and after 4 nightes of Hard marching never
travveled in a road Jouus at night on the fifth day we come into
London Ky whear the government had a recruiting Station thear
was the Stars and Stripes on a big flag pole we marched around
that with our hates off chering for Uncle Sam*

David and his brothers were just one part of an amazing exodus.
Estimates vary, but it is generally conceded that between twenty
thousand and thirty thousand men slipped out of East Tennessee and
made their way into Kentucky to escape conscription in the Confederate army or certain prison. Not all were as lucky as the Haworth
boys. One group of four hundred young men and boys from the New
Market area were captured just forty miles from home by a regiment
of East Tennessee Confederate Cavalry. They were sent to prison.[5]

The Confederates did their best to intercept this flow of potential
recruits.

HDQRS. DEPARTMENT OF EAST TENNESSEE, Knoxville, April 18,
1862. Col. JOHN C. VAUGHN, Cmdg., &c., Kingston, Tenn.:
COL.: The major-general commanding directs me to inform
you that large numbers of Union men are leaving this and adjoining
counties, intending to go through the passes of the Cumberland into
Kentucky. He directs that all the disposable cavalry of your command
be sent with the utmost dispatch to operate between Clinton and the
north valley of Powell's River and intercept them in their attempt.
Few of them are armed.

You will give the officer commanding the cavalry instructions to attack and disperse these men wherever they may be found.

Very respectfully, your obedient servant, H. L. CLAY, Assistant Adjutant-Gen[6]

Joseph Lamb was more unlucky than most.

About the 9th of August, I together with Calvin Garrett, William Martin and Joel B. Crawford, now confined in prison with me at Camp Chase, with many others left our homes in Knox and Union Counties and started for Kentucky to unite with the Federal Army, then lying at or near Camp Dick Robinson. After traveling all night and the forenoon of the next day, having arrived at the foot of the Cumberland Mountains and about thirty miles on our journey, our advance was attacked by a squad of secession cavalry under command of Capt. Ashby. We were unarmed. Capt. Thornburg, of our party, was wounded in the neck and he and nine others taken prisoners. We were informed by the mountain pilots that it would be impossible to cross the Confederate lines, they being too closely guarded, upon which we all returned to our homes, narrowly escaping being taken prisoners upon our return.[7]

Eventually the Confederate authorities forced Lamb into their army. His wife secretly provided him with a white handkerchief that he planned to wave at the first sign of Union troops. His plan worked perfectly except for one thing: The Union soldiers took him as a Confederate prisoner and sent him to a Union prison camp where he spent the next months trying to convince someone that he was, actually, a patriotic Union citizen. There is no record of how his efforts turned out.

Fortunately the Haworth brothers escaped all that.

Comeing down the mountain that after noon we struck a man on a mule with a Sack of dried apples. I had on Bootes and feet was Scalded and Sore from wadeing the Creekes I gave the man a half doller to let me ride. Had the sack of apples in frunt & no Saddle

the way was pretty steap Jouust a trail the mule got scard stuck his
hed Down & humped his back so I had nothing too hold too so I
went on and landed up against a big Bolder and skined my head
some. I got up and walked the rest of the way prettey good. The
next morning I couldent get my boots on and they was calling for
all men that wanted to join the armey to get in line I went out
in my sock feet and lined up when the Officer come down to me
and James N. Northern we told him that we wanted to join the
armey ountill the Southern army was whiped if it took 10 years he
said he couldn't enlist us that way he would enlist us for 3 years or
deureing the war evrey man that got in line and wanted to join
the army was sworn in. That way no boddey was examed

When the Haworth brothers and their friends signed their enlistment papers they were, in a sense, putting a period to their part in a doctrine that had been troubling the Quakers for more than two hundred years. It was spelled out by George Fox, founder of the Quaker movement, in 1610:

"We utterly deny all outward wars and strife and fighting with outward weapons for any end or under any pretence, whatever. This is our testimony to the whole world."

They held to this belief and, in many circles, were admired for it. But then there was the question of slavery. Quakers were the first to oppose human slavery and the first to require their members to free their slaves. But there was no agreement on how to deal with the issue as it existed throughout the country. Some wanted to push for immediate abolition; others felt it would be best to appeal to reason, even urging slaves to obey their masters and wait for a more enlightened time. Quakers were pacifists and had no desire to become revolutionaries, and many feared that a rash approach might instigate armed conflict. The disagreement finally led to a split between those who advised patience and those who wanted immediate action. Another group developed a belief that each individual should be governed by his or her own conscience and not by some external authority.

Quakers in the South tried using what they called "disinterested benevolence," a kind of polite appeal to authorities, but the reaction to their appeals became so violent that thousands of Friends were forced out of Virginia, the Carolinas, and Georgia, a migration that would eventually be repeated in East Tennessee.

Then, as the Southern states began seceding, another cause sprang up: the preservation of the Union. Many men, including some Quakers who were not ready to fight to free slaves, were persuaded to fight for that cause. One survey at the time estimated that 25 to 62 percent of young Quaker men in Indiana fought in the war. David's "cheering for Uncle Sam pretty good" suggests that preserving the Union might have been one reason Quakers from this region of the country enlisted. But there can be no doubt their primary goal was to escape the Confederate draft. They had accomplished that at considerable peril and were now in Uncle Sam's army. It would be difficult to remain pacifist when other men were trying to kill you.

> [April 15, 1862]
> *on the 15th of April we marched up to flat lick Ky and was mustered intoo the 3rd Tenn Infantry and our squad orgnized as Co K and we Elected Wm. A. Sawyers as Captain Nat Peck as first Lieut Wm C. Haworth 2cd lieut Wm M. Lewis First Sargt D.M. Haworth 2cd Sargt*

And so David's older brother William entered service as an officer, and David as second sergeant.

> [April 24, 1862]
> *On the 24 we had preaching by the chaplin in the fore noon then I was sent out acros the river with a scout we brought in one prisner & comeing in to the landing our canoo uppset and put us all in the river we lost one gun we remained in camp ountill Drilling most evrey day and garding the road towardes Cumberlan gap*

The first mention of the Third Tennessee Infantry in the official records came on April 24, 1862, when Brigadier General James Spears, commanding the Twenty-Fifth Brigade of the Army of the Ohio at Boston, Kentucky, requested that the regiment be sent to reinforce him. At the time Colonel Leonidas C. Houk was the regiment's commander.

[May 5, 1862]
Sunday May the 5th we was working the road all day and it araining. Sunday night the regment was called out and double quicked up to Cumberland ford our Co was put out to gard the telegraph line

[May 11, 1862]
On May 11th we marched all day and camped that night at Roberston church

[May 12, 1862]
On the 12th we was out on a scout and captured 4 prisners.

[May 13–17 1862]
On the 13 we started on a fors march marched 30 miles went into camp at Williamsburg Crost the state line on the 15th into Tenn at 3 oclock and on the 17th we located Camp at Pinat Tenn

[May 18, 1862]
May 18th Being in camp at Pinat and it Being Sunday we had preaching by the chaplin

[May 22, 1862]
and on the 22cd we went on a scout Across pine Mountain Ike being sick he was left in camp we returned the same night

[May 26, 1862]
on Monday May 26 we moved out in the direction of big creek gap and was met a lot of rebel cav in about 3 mile of the gap this was our first engagement but we soon drove them back to the gap

[May 28, 1862]
on the 28 of May we struck tentes and marched out by Bosten we then ordered back to our old camp at Pinat whear we staid ountill the 1st of June

[June 1, 1862]
We struck tentes on the 1st and marched out and that night we camped on muddey Creek

[June 2, 1862]
And on the 2cd we camped at landmans gap whear we staid ountill the 6 when we again broke camp and marched out

[June 7, 1862]
and on the 7th we went into camp at Pinat

[June 11, 1862]
on the 11th we marched out and crosed pine mountain and made camp that night in Big Creek Gap

[June 12, 1862]
On the night of the 11 our reg made a forst march to hunters gap reaching thear jous before daylight. we had two citicen gides Col Bradford with his regment of Cav was camp in a hollow near a spring we closed in on them and had them all surrounded but one road down the Hollow they was geteing thear Breakfast aiming to come and drive us out of the gap we closed in on them in a charge we killed some of them and captured the most of them after the fight was over we gathered up the food and had a good Breakfast returning to our camp in big creek Gap

[June 14, 1862]
and on the 14th June the confederates drove in our picketes and that night the rest of our Brigade come up under General Spears

[June 15, 1862]
*the next day we set a trap for them placed a lot of troopes on one
side of the road behind the rocks sent out a squad of our Cav and
opened up a fit with the enemy then retreated and drawed them
in we got the most of them a few that hadn't got in too far got out
our Brigade had the 1,2,3,4,5, & 6 Tenn regmentes commanded
by General Spears we started up on the South side of the mountain for Cumberland gap we was reinforsed at Williams Gap by
infantrey and artilrey before we reached the gap*

[June 21, 1862]
*Late on the 21ˢᵗ of June the Enemy had fled and we marched in
witheout aney fighting long Tom a big canon was on a high part
of the mountain East of the gap they spiked him with a rattail file
then Roled him off of the mountain. all the rest of the artilerry
was spiked and the spokes hafed intoo* [halved in two] *between
the rim and hub. We captured a lot Flower* [flour] *Bacon and
other provisions*

[July 4, 1862]
*July 4 struck tents and marched out 2 miles south went into camp
2 ½ miles up in lea Co Virginia at Camp Morgan Col Bob Johnson made a speach to the town soldiers*

[July 7, 1862]
*On the 7ᵗʰ our reg went out near Tazewell forageing Marched
back in side of the picket line and camped Come to camp the next
morning*

[July 14, 1862]
*July 14ᵗʰ Broke camp and marched through Cumberlan Gap and
on Sunday we crosed log Mountain.*

[July 16, 1862]
on the 16ᵗʰ we marched hard all day and camped on Big Creek

[July 17, 1862]
*on the morning of the 17th we started for Walises Cross roades we
piled our knapsacs up in the woodes and left them varey warm
and no watter on the double quick and run me and Ike gave out
I was sunstroke dident no what was gowing on for quite awhile
when I come too Ike and Jim Northern had got me out in the
Brush away from the road and had gone and ^found^ a Branch
and got some watter then we got Back too our knapsacs and staid
thear ountill our reg come back then we returned back to our old
Camp Morgan*

[July 20, 1862]
*July 20th being in Camp Morgan we had preaching again then
Genrel Spears and Generel Thewit [Lt. Col. Daniel C. Trewhitt?] made speaches to the Tenn soldiers We are ordered back
intoo Kentuckey Dont want to go Expected to go into Tenn*

The men had good reasons for wanting to go back into East Tennessee.
Reports of the conditions there had undoubtedly reached them, and they
would have been fearful for the families they had left behind. One report,
sent some months earlier by the Reverend William Blount Carter, was
typical.

This whole country is in a wretched condition, a perfect despotism
reigns here. The Union men of East Tennessee are longing and pray-
ing for the hour when they can break their fetters. The loyalty of our
people increases with the oppressions they have to bear. Men and
women weep for joy when I merely hint to them that the day of our
deliverance is at hand. I have not seen a secession flag since I entered
the State. I beg you to hasten on to our help as we are about to create
a great diversion in Gen. McClellan's favor. It seems to me if you
would ask if he would spare at once 5,000 or 10,000 well-drilled
troops. Will you not ask for more help?

Wm. Blount Carter[8]

But despite all the pleas for help from many quarters, including President Lincoln himself, there would be no Union troops headed for East Tennessee for many months. This was a bitter disappointment to the patriotic residents there. It meant they would have to put up with their Confederate occupiers, many of whom had a decidedly negative opinion of East Tennessee. One Alabama volunteer expressed it in a lengthy letter to a friend in Mobile.

August 25, 1862.
You see from the date of my letter that we have moved east. We are near Cumberland Gap, and right in a nest of Unionists and abolitionists. We have had no fighting yet, but from present prospects I think we will have some work very soon. This is the poorest, meanest country I ever stopped in, and the people are poorer and meaner than the country. I have been scouting a good many miles from the camp and find that the further I go the worse they get. The women are large, healthy, strong, ugly and stupid; they wear only one garment, and that sets as close to them as a pair of pantaloons. The men are entirely worthy of the women. How they live here is a mystery to me. I see but a few patches of corn, and that will all be made into whisky. An immense crowd of the nation visits our camp every day, bringing from a quart to a half gallon of buttermilk (from ten miles sometimes), and a dozen or so Irish potatoes, which they sell at famine prices or barter for bacon.

We find the latter article a better circulating medium than the Tennessee bills, with which we were paid off at Union City. There is not enough silver in this country to break a ten dollar note. We get rid of our money, however, among ourselves, with the aid of "set back" and "draw poker." Card playing is almost the only amusement we have at present. There has been so much rain lately, that, except when on duty, we are obliged to stick in our tents and play, to prevent death from ennui.

To-day is Sunday, and in the distance I hear some psalm singing, and presume from that fact that the chaplain is on duty. That gentleman up to this time has found his office a sinecure. The first two or three times he held forth, quite a crowd went to hear him, but at present, to use the language of a flush messmate of mine, "the thing's played out . . ."

Item: Two women have just passed through the camp—best I have seen yet— low neck, short sleeve, short frock, (latter too much so by twenty inches.) The weather has cleared up and the sun is coming down at the rate of 99 Fahrenheit. I stopped writing to make a chicken trade with the females I mentioned above. I got ten chickens from the biggest footed one for two dollars and "nine pence." That is the best trade that has been made since we got here. I flatter myself that exterior had a good deal to do with it. I also contracted with her for one gallon of buttermilk and five pounds of butter to be delivered to-morrow at the rate of 50 cents per gallon of milk and 20 cents per pound of butter, (a tip-top contract.) I'd like to have you dine with me to-morrow. At all the places where we have camped the ladies have come in crowds to see us. Many of them have been very kind and have tried to make themselves useful, particularly about the sick, but it's no go. I was a little sick while at Corinth and was visited by some seven or eight, armed with soup, tea, arrow root and other fixings, together with advice, consolation, &c. I can say, from experience, that they did no good on my case. I could not help feeling very much bothered while they were talking to me and of course was too polite to refuse taking anything they offered, and always thanked them profusely.

The result is my system is still thoroughly saturated with arrowroot, &c., and I have almost lost all taste for mustard, pepper, salt, &c., from having suffered a great quantity of the former condiment to be extensively used in my case, at the earnest request of some ladies who were treating me. I would not have used any of the stuff, but they promised to call again and I was afraid they would catch me.[9]

An unknown editorial writer in Nashville, then in Union hands, saw the situation quite differently.

What is to Become of the East Tennesseans?
The above inquiry is one of grave importance, and the urgent necessity for a prompt answer is made manifest by the wasted farms and pillaged houses of thousands of the loyal citizens of this neglected section.

Our farms are wantonly laid waste, all our horses and cattle are taken unnecessarily, all the hogs killed that will do to eat, and the stock hogs shot down to prevent us from raising more.

Our best farmers will not be able to start a single plow when spring comes, and if they had the horses they have nothing to feed them on. In such a condition of things, what is to become of a population of near one hundred and fifty thousand women and children? It is a high time we had some intimation of the policy of the Government towards the loyal people of East Tennessee.

This appeal, however, to East Tennesseans to stand by their colors, is superfluous, as they are unconditional Union men, and cannot be driven from duty by the thieves who rob their families, nor by the jeers of irresponsible, cowardly letter writers, who are continually writing to Northern journals about their ignorance, nor by that "most unkindest cut of all"—the charge of cowardice.[10]

Whether or not they were mindful of the national debate about their homes, there was nothing for David and the Third Tennessee but to keep marching.

[July 20, 1862]
July the 20 we broke camp and marched out gowing north at 2 oclock I gave out on the mountain and W C Haworth and myself was sent too the hospitel ~~whear~~ wehear we staid ountill the 26 when one hundred of us in command of Lieut James Miser of Co G started to join our regment my Brother was not able to travel and was left at the hospitel Marched all day camped at Cumberlan ford and on the 31ˢᵗ we found our regment in camp at Lundun Kentuckey they was camped in and Around the Brick School Hous

[August 3, 1862]
August 3 in camp all day

[August 4, 1862]
on the 4th we left camp went as gardes for some Artilrey that was gowing to Cumberland gap

[August 6, 1862]

on the 6th we camped in a big orchard at the edge of Barbersvill Ky Ike being sick with the yellow Jaunders I brought him up in one of the wagons other troopes Took the wagon train on and Remained in camp

[August 8, 1862]

At sundown on the 8 we broke camp and started back gardeing another wagon train Joust at night we come intoo our old Camp at Lundun all supplies for the armey at Cumberland Gap has to be hauled up in wagons from Lexinton Ky and we are garde^ing^ the road

[August 10, 1862]

on Sunday the 10th I went out with Tom Northern and Jeff Troutman in the countrey forageing for some hay

[August 13, 1862]

on the 13th Captin McNish and myself went 7 miles North East after a rebel Bushwhacker but couldent locate him Comeing back I sprained my Ankle and the captain had to get a man with a hors to bring me to camp

[August 16, 1862]

on the 16th I was detailed by Col L.C. Houlke to take a dispatch to Lieutenent Col Coffe Childes whoo was stationed at Richmond Ky with half of our reg Berrey Hadsel our commissary Sargent let me have his sorrel mare the Colonel gave me his navey [a model of the popular Colt revolver].*^as^ I rode out of the school hous groundes the ^Col^ said it was 20 minetes till 9 oclock A.M. and the Col told me if my mare gave out to take another one Joust after noon I came to a little clearing an orchard and hous back of it and a log stable clost too the road and a good lookeing hors tied with the saddle on so I thought I [untelligible] get him. I slide off steped over the lot fence and ountide him and joust as I steped out of the stable doore a big long* *whiskered fellow steped around the coner with a double barel shot gun with boath hamers back and his fingers dangerus near the trigers he said turn that hors loos and I droped the haulter he said whear doo you belong I told him to the 3ʳᵈ Tenn next was whear is your reg I said right down the road then he said get out of hear so I stepped prettey brisk. And I spurred up my mare and kept looking Back I think he was a bushewhacker and would have killed me if he had known the factes I rode into Col childes camp on the west side of richmon Ky before sun down and delivered my message*

[August 17, 1862]
On the 17ᵗʰ the command broke camp and started for Lundon about dalight it being Sunday I rode on ahead but my mare was so worn that I couldent travel fast I stop at Wᵐ Coils to get some diner he lived up on the big hill I hitched my mare at the gate and while eateing diner some one come runing in and said that Scootes Confederate Cave was come down the lane I ran out to the frunt and saw that they was too close for me to get my mare. I told Mr. Coils Boy to take my saddle and briddle ^in^ and hide them and turn the mare in the field Lieut Sphel Dave Myers Louie Barns and my self ran back by the stabels and followed down a branch keepeing in the brush and big Weedes we sucseded in reaching the woodes without being discovered by the Enemy My self and Lieut Safel sit down on a log and watched about five hundred of Scotes Cav pass by after sundown we started out and we came to a hous and the ladey gave us sumething to eat She was lookeing for her husband to come thought he belonged to that command so we went back intoo the timber and slep

While Sgt. Haworth was off on his mission, Confederate Major General Kirby Smith began an invasion of Kentucky. Col. Houk was attacked by the Confederates under Col. John S. Scott. Scott's cavalry was probably part of that attack. The Union troops were driven out of London, and Col. Scott reported killing thirteen, wounding seventeen, and capturing

III of Houk's command. Col. Houk reported that he escaped into the woods with about two hundred men.[11] In the meantime, Sgt. Haworth was cut off from his unit.

[August 18, 1862]
The nexte morning we went back and after watching around awhile I couldent find aney hors so we went in and she got us up a good meal we then ^we^ traveled on about 2 mile but the rebels was scattered over the countey It was dangerus for us to go aney further so we went to a hous and the man was a union man so he Kept us hid away ountill the 21. Col Medcalf & Col Childes haveing come up to the foot of the big hill the rebels having fell back

[August 22, 1862]
on the 22 I went Back to Coiles and got my mare and joined Col Childes at camp at Newlins at the foot o big hill

[August 23, 1862]
Augus 23 Sargt Wm N. Lewis and John Naples come too us we was camped on a branch joust south of Mr. Newlins hous I tide my mar to a saplin and fed her never sean her aney more about one oclock the battle of big hill commenced betwean Medcalfs Cav and Scotes Cav. we was ordered out to support them when we started out I had no gun but meeteing one of Medcalfs Cav shot through the right arm I got his gun and ammunition our command had 72 men under Col Childes Right at the foot of big hill we met Medcalfs troopes in full retreat with the ^rebels^ slashing them Col childes formed his men on a little ridge faceing the road that went up the hill and when our troopes past we pored a volley intoo the rebel cav that tumbled off 8 or ten in the road and we kept it up ountill the rest of them got clear back up the hill and oute of range. One boy that fell off pretty close to me had a letter showing from his coat pocket I took it out and I found the following ritten on the last page of the letter joust like I put it hear

Henrey
May sorrows never thy path way cross
Nor trouble bligt thy hart so free
May thou never sufer friendships loss
Nor drain the cup of misery
But may fair fortun on the smile
And peas thy gidelight be
To shield the[e] while on earth from gilt
And fit the[e] for Eternitey
C A C
Cotage home March 15th 1861

August 23 we fell in and started back down the ^road^ we hadent gotten to Newlins hous when we sean ^the rebels^ comeing down the road Medcalfs had all gone left us we climb over the fence and started for a creek not fure off the fence was big flat post were set in the ground and holes mortised in the post each end flatened and sliped in tight was hard to tare down we put severel of them out while they was working at it from that on ountill night set in and we kept up a lively fight the ^creak^ was varey crooked and rail fences along the bank we wold lay down behind the bank the old Col kept talking to us telling us to keep cool and not shoot ountill he giv us the ^order^ then for every man to shoot the one right in frunt and not to shot a hors get the rider and the hors would run off some times we would cross the creek back and forth so they couldent get at us varey good Joust as the sun was gowing down we made our last stand whear we struck the turnpike we give them a good farwell but we had to go they had a lot of them went down the turnpike road and come around in our rear the creek hear was over waist deep and I stoped to load my gun all our boyes had gone over & joust as I put the cap on one of them brod brim^ed^ hat fellows had slip along up and had his hors nearley on too me before I noticed him he fired at me with his revolver the bulit brushed my hare over my left Ear But the next shot was mine I never put my ^gun^ to my shoulder just turned the muzel up pretty clost to his left side and pulled the triger he droped his revolver in the ^creek^ and he tumbled off then I made a run for the other side thear was a little boddey ^of^ timber I could see that they had captured Col Childes and his bunch that was with him So I started as hard as I could run across and old field that had gowed up in sproutes and briars trying to get to the timber on the other side but about 25 of them put in after ^me^ ashooting and yelling It looked like I dident have much chance to get thear It joust struck me that I might fool them so I fell flat on my face and laid still like I was killed the horses jumped over they went on after some more of our boyes and ^I^ shoved my ^gun^ under some sproutes and I crawled under a big bunch and lay thear ountill it got dark then I got out and started for a Big farm hous at the edge of the timber I struck one of our boyes when we got clost to the hous I heard some one in the ^hous^ taken on like he was hurt I told this man to stay out thear and listen I went in I found one of our boyes laying on the ^flour^ shot through he couldent talk and I got a pillow and put under his head tride to give him some water but he couldent swallow it my man outside called and I went ^out^ thear was a squade of thear Cav come^ing^ down the fence the people that lived thear had all gone we slip around the barn and got away went out in the timber away from aney road piled up some leaves against a log and went to sleap

The Third Tennessee won a commendation from Major General William Nelson for this action and the citation gives some interesting details of the battle.

> On Saturday, August 23, the 7th Kentucky Cavalry, under Colonel Metcalfe, together with a battalion of Houk's 3rd Tennessee Regiment, under Lieutenant Colonel Chiles, attacked the enemy at Big Hill, Rockcastle County. Colonel Metcalfe led the attack with much gallantry, but had the mortification to find that not more than 100 of his regiment followed him; the remainder, at the first cannon shot, turned tail and fled like a pack of cowards. The conduct of the Tennessee battalion presents a refreshing contrast to the foregoing.

They met the enemy bravely, checked his advance, rescued Colonel Metcalfe, abandoned by his own regiment, and though too few to retrieve the action, at least saved the honor of our arms. Lieutenant Colonel Chiles will accept the thanks of the Major General and convey to his officers and men his high appreciation of their gallantry and good conduct.

[August 24, 1862]
The next morning the 24 of August We started out to find some place whear we could get something to eat we struck a little field & big road on the oposit side I had started to climb over when the word rang out Surrender I tumbled back on the ground Joust as the rebel picket fired we struck off down a hollow in the timber and run ountill we give out then we set down and this boy was crying he was beging me to go back and surrender I tride to get ^him^ out of that notion but ^he^ left me right thear and went back in the direction of the rebel picket I never heard of him aney more. I came back to William queans and he kept me hid and feed me ountill Thursday when I started out and travelled on to richmond Ky whear we staid ountill the 29 when we could hear heavey canonadeing out ^too the^ frunt

The battalion was held in the rear during the battle for Richmond and did not take part in the main fighting. They were engaged with Confederate cavalry during the retreat from Richmond. Eleven officers and twenty-seven men, including Lieutenant Colonel Chiles, were reported missing or captured.

[August 30, 1862]
and on Sadurday the 30th the fightting was heavey all day I had bin sick ever since comeing in late in the ^day^ Managed to get out in town the ^rebels^ was driveing our men through town so I started out down the pike but was too weak to walk findeing

one of our wagons with the tung broke and the saddle mule gone
I drop the tuges loost the gee stick of the lead mule and Jumped on
him he sure done some bucking but ^I^ clinched my heales and
helt to the hames he was gowing in the right Direction Joust as
I come out the rebel Cav closed in from boath sides and captured
all of them I got to the Kentucky river joust at dark and found an
old darky he took me and the mule down home with ^him^ and
an old ant doctored me up thear was 5 hundred of our inft camped
on the north side of the Kentuckey river the next morning before
I got across the river they broke camp and started on the retreat I
had found John Maples of my co when we got across the river we
had to travel back away from the road old John Morgan was on
the road

A Confederate cavalry under Colonel John Hunt Morgan, who was eventually promoted to brigadier general, was part of a force led by Confederate General Kirby Smith that was attempting to capture all of Kentucky. By the first of September the Kentucky legislature had already adjourned and headed for a more secure location.

[September 1, 1862]
on the first day of September we walked into Main street in
Lexington Ky joust about sundown after the town had bin sur-
*rendered to John Morgan our troopes had all gone we could ^see^*
Morgans troopes comeing in ^too^ the south end of mane St Joust
then a omnibus with 4 god horses came up the streat he was trying
to save his horses I steped out to the middle of the streat with my
navey in my hand and stoped him He said his buss was ful I told
Maples to get in I climbed up and rode with the driver He drove
hard we reached Williamsburg sometime after midnight and w
slept on the flour at the Hotel on the corner we had a wagon train
in camp

[September 1862]

Joust below town joust at daylight I herd cav passing I looked out and saw five hundred of Morgans cav gowing by in a trot None of them stoped in town they was after that wagon train as soon as the all got by me and ^Maples^ started travilling NorthEast kept away from the main roades and we arrived at Covington Ky on the 6

[September 8, 1862]

and on the 8th we crost the ohio river into Cincinnetia we staid with the cittey patroles

There was great fear that the Confederates were preparing to invade Cincinnati. The militia had been called out to defend the city.

[September 13, 1862]

on the 13th I was standeing on the streat lookeing at some New troopes pasing Some of them called my name and I went out too them It was the 73 Ills Inft I went with them Across the river and they camped in the South Edge of Covington I new Capt McNut and most of his Co I drilled his Co evrey day the ^first^ drilling that the had

[September 15, 1862]

on the 15 we moved camp went across Lick creek too the left wing drilling evrey day on the 18th we crosed back across the ohio river

[September 19, 1862]

on the 19th we was loaded otoo a steam boat bound for Lewisville Ky which place we reached the next night the boat tied up and we staid abord ountill the morning of the 20 then we marched out through town and camped on the Lewisvill and Nashville R R

[September 21, 1862]
*and the 21 being Sunday we tended preaching after which we
went on fatieug dutey diging riful pites*

[September 23, 1862]
*On the 23ʳᵈ we moved inside of the the workes the wimin and
children are all ordered to move out side the citey all of the brigade
stay in the Rifel pites evrey night*

[September 24, 1862]
*On the ^24^ we moved camp Located out east of town near the
water workes I went out and found Majer Cross with part of my
regiment I found joust 2 of my co Sargt Wᵐ M Lewis and John
Maples I staid with them the next day was Sunday. we was on
piket all day*

[October 1, 1862]
*we was ordered out at 3 oclock the morning of October 1ˢᵗ drawed 3
dayes rations and w started for perreyvill Generl Buel in command of the army the Entire army is moveing the first day we
marched through Jeffersonton the second day we past through
Millvill and Taylersville and Bloomfield and on Sunday we had
some picket fighting on Monday we marched hard all day and
camped on Chaplin river*

[October 7, 1862]
on the 7 we camped at Maxville [Possibly Mackville, Ken-
tucky]

[October 8, 1862]
*Oct the 8th the long rool was beat before dailight we marched out
formed battle line then we piled up our knapsacks and evrey thing
But our gunes Cateridg box & canteen we moved over to support
the left wing which was soon hard presed by the rebel Inft. we
joined in with the 32 Ky inft and took a position behind Turels
Batery whear we lay down this was about 11 oclock we hadn't*

bin thear long ountil we was with fixed Bayonetes ordered to charge and when we reached the top of ~~the~~ whear the batterry was stationed we could sea the rebel line of infantry comeing in a charge we loaded and fired into them as fast as we could. we couldent stop them the Artilrey men so maney of them haveing bin killed or wounded thear hardly men enuf to man the gunes I saw Generl Terrel leave his hors [General Terrill was mortally wounded in the battle] *the man that ramed the load down was shot [unintelligible] tooke his place and staid ountill the rebels killed him and when they had taken the batterry we was ordered to retreat. my self and W^m M Lewis being clost together we ran down the Sloap a little wayes and we boath stoped behind a big tree. we was in a blew gras pasture, joust a few large trees. we was loadeing and shooting as fast as we could. the rebels had turned our Battery on us and was giveing ^us^ some shells one burst in the top of our tree seamed to tare the top out the limbes falling around us the nouyse was turable so much artilrey and musketery could hardly hear each other talk I felt Lewis on the ground strugeling I looked down at him I thought by his actions and lookes that he was about Killed he soon lay still I kept on loadeing ^and^ and shooting as fast as I could. I think I had fired about 3 times after he was nocked down when I felt him stru- geling trying to get up he would partley ^get^ up then fall down. He had bin struck on the head and was all Bloodey I set my ^gun^ down and got holt under his arms and lifted him up holding ^him^ against the tree ountill he got steady after a little while I said "Can you walk" he thought he could I saw that the rebels was lineing up to make another charge I told him to get backe to the rear he started sloley. I watched him as he went off he was varey bowleged and I saw a shell or solid shot strike the ground a little wayes behind him rebound and went through betwean bills leges I did not stay long I loaded and pulled down strait on one ^of^ them I started down the hill It was pretty thick young timber in the Little valey when I got in thear I ran intoo a lot of Morgans Cave that had come around the left flank and was geteing a lot of our Boys. I dodged through them and got past them without geteing hurt. I kept runing up through a cornfield and joust at the top of the Ridge I saw twenty four peases of ^our^ artilerry comeing in with the horses on the gallop unlimbered and pored shot and shell intoo the rebel infantrey that was comeing up the slope in a charge they never stoped come right on and I joust stood thear and watched the battle. I was so famished for water that I could not talk. the night before the battle we camped by a big pond. before we started I went to fill my canteen and I saw a dead mule lying in the edge of the pond so I dident get much water. the rebes continued to come but seamed to be geteing slower and slower. they got so close that our inft support raised up and fixed Bayonetes when the rebels stoped joust a minet then broke and retreated but the ground was covered with gray coates that Never went back. I staid ountill the battle was over and looked over the field that was the first battle that I had had a good view of and our artilrey did the work fine, and late in the day when it was nearley dark I found John Maples and 2 other boys of our reg. we started to the rear to hunt some water. we didn't go far until we struck some rebel cave and they cut ^us^ off from our army so we traveled all night trying to find our reg*

This was the battle of Perryville, fought between Confederate General Braxton Bragg and Union General Don Carlos Buell.

The battle of Perryville was the most important battle fought in Kentucky. It forced the Confederates to give up their plans for conquering that state and to retreat southward into East Tennessee.

[October 9, 1862]
on the 9th we traveled all day through the timer and fieldes away from the pike and that night we staide all night with Martin Young

[October 11, 1862]
on the 11th we took up a deserter from the 19th ohio reg we traveld

*hard all Day we past close to Thompsonville we got tirred
bothering with the deserter so we turned him loose. we struck the
bloomfield pike 6 miles below Springfield that nigh we slep in an
oates pen then we crost the turn pike and tooke breakfast with
Mr. Grigesby we then traveled on crosing chaplin river and had
diner ^with^ old Jacob Ward and that night we staid with John
Glass and the next day being Monday we staid all day with Mr.
Glass and all went squirl hunteing and remained over Monday
night resteing up*

[October 14, 1862]
*on the 14 we again took diner with our friend Jacob Ward then
started on went around Chaplin Struck the Bloomfield pike one
mile below come on to Talorsville and staid all night at the Spen-
cer hotel we past throgh Fishersville and Brownstown staid all
night 2 miles below with John McCarneys*

[October 17, 1862]
*on the 17 marched into Lewisville Ky and got transportation to
Cincincinattia ohio Crost the ohiow river to Jeffersonville Got
on the train that night at 10 oclock changed cars at Semore left
thear at 7 oclock arrived in Cincincinnata and went to the citey
barracks to await transportation too our part of the reg which
had come back with Generel George W Morgan when he vacated
Cumberland Gap Ky and was now in camp at Galifoleas ohio
the old captan in charge of the patrol gardes being short of men
wanted to keep us with him wouldent send us out in the city for
fear that we get some way to go too our reg we had bin cooped
up thear in the uper roomes for 3 days I got a Dailey papers and
I saw that Col Bill Brownlow was registerest at a hotell I rote a
note to him and watched for a newes boy put 25 cts in it and call
one and droped it down and told him to deliver it to the Col it
wasent but a few hours ountill the col come intoo the office and
called for us the old captain was a ruff old man he wanted to now
hoo the col was that should aske him as to his command I was in
the next rom and I heard the col I come out then called Mapples*

> *the col told the old capt to take our names off of his booke he*
> *would take charge of us and we went out of that place as happey*
> *as if we was gowing home the col tooke us first to a barber shop*
> *had a shave har cut and bath then we got on a streat car and the*
> *col tooke me and John Maples too his fathers home old Parson*
> *Brownlow whear we staid all night*

William G. (Parson) Brownlow was one of the most prominent oppo-
nents of Tennessee's secession from the union. In addition to being an
ordained minister he was a journalist, published his own newspaper,
and used its columns to attack the proponents of secession throughout
that debate. Once Tennessee left the Union the Confederate authorities
had Brownlow arrested and prepared to put him on trial for treason. He
appealed for his release, much to the disgust of many southerners, including J.G.M. Ramsey, who protested to President Jefferson Davis.

KNOXVILLE, TENN., December 7, 1861. Hon. JEFFERSON DAVIS,
President Confederate States of America.

SIR: The Confederate civil authorities here had Mr. Brownlow
arrested last evening under a charge of treason. He is now in jail. It
is understood that parties in this place are taking or perhaps have
already taken, measures to apply for executive clemency in his behalf,
and turn him at large or transfer him under a military escort to the
enemy's lines in Kentucky. To this course we enter our most respect-
ful but decided protest and remonstrance . . . the proposition to
release the prime mover and instigator of all this rebellion against the
South and Tennessee and send him an authorized emissary to the
headquarters of the enemy dignified with an escort of our Tennessee soldiery has startled this community, embracing in the number
citizens and most of the army here. The feeling of indignation at the
bare effort for his release is much intensified by the fact which as it
may not be fully known at Richmond we take leave to bring to your
attention, viz, that the prisoner shortly before the burning of our
railroad bridges and other acts of incendiarism and disloyalty had left
town and visited Blount and Sevier Counties, the residence of the
malcontents who are known as the incendiaries, and the suspicion is

widely entertained that he prompted and instigated that and other atrocities. This peregrination into the most disloyal and disaffected neighborhoods makes him the more familiar with the extent of the disaffection—their plans, purposes, &c.

A more dangerous and more capable emissary could not be found in the Southern Confederacy to stimulate invasion of Tennessee and advise and carry into effect every kind of mischief. His arrival in Kentucky and Lincolndom generally would be hailed as a greater achievement than the capture of Zollicoffer and his brave troops.

Portrait of Parson Brownlow. *Courtesy Library of Congress, LC-DIG-ppmsca-35561.*

We do not deem it necessary to enlarge further on the subject but we earnestly advise against the proposed release and transportation to Kentucky. Let the civil or military law take its course against the criminal leader in this atrocious rebellion as it has already done to his deluded and ignorant followers.

We have the honor to be, very respectfully, your obedient servants,

J. G. M. RAMSEY

WM. H. Tibbs[7]

Despite such protests Brownlow was eventually released and escorted under military guard to Cincinnati, where he continued to promote the Union cause and assist such Union soldiers as came his way, including David Haworth.

He apparently continued his journalistic efforts, at one time incurring the wrath of General Sherman, who carried on his own private war with reporters throughout the Civil War.

HDQRS. MILITARY DIVISION OF THE MISSISSIPPI, Nashville, April 2, 1864.

Gen. SCHOFIELD, Knoxville:

Your dispatch is received, and is very satisfactory. I will telegraph its substance to Washington.

The Cincinnati papers of the 1st contain dispatches announcing that Buell is to supersede you. There is no truth in this. The report seems to have originated at Chattanooga, and I have telegraphed to Thomas to punish the operator.

The papers also contain a message from Knoxville giving my movements, and gives a message from Parson Brownlow to the effect that the rebels will certainly invade Kentucky by Pound Gap. Tell Parson Brownlow that he must leave military matters to us, and that he must not chronicle my movements or those of any military body. If he confines his efforts to his own sphere of action he will do himself more credit and his country more good.

W. T. SHERMAN, Maj.-Gen.[12]

Whether Parson took Sherman's advice is not recorded.

> *the old parson seamed as glad too sea us as if We was his boyes he new my father before the ware we ^heard^ his daughter play the piano that kept 6 Rebel soldiers from pulling the Stares and Stripes down at thear home in Knoxville Tenn withe a six shooter leveled on them General Carter staid all night thear the next morning Col Brownlow got transportation four us and send us up with Generel Carter that night we got too Portland ohio on the ohio river Staid all night started early next morning walked too Galopoleas got thear at dark found our co with part of our reg we had bin separated four 3 monthes I being the second sargt Wm M Lewis not being with the co he was ordly Sargt and I had to take his place the command was camped on the banke of the ohio River*

above Galipolies our command was paid off for six monthes and
19 dayes I drawed one hundred and twelve dollers and seventey
five centes

[November 8, 1862]
November 8 snowed all day and was varey cold

[November 9, 1862]
the next day was Sunday. James K. Ritche of Georgetown Ills vis-
ited with us all day and I loned his companey $80⁰⁰ In camp all
day the boys all had plentey of money and were haveing a big time
3 Jewes come intoo our camp selling the boys cheap watches at a
big price Generl Spears head of them he sent out the patrol gardes
and had them brought to his headquarters which was on the bank
of the river he had the gardes to make the 3 Jews wade out intoo
the river ountill the water was up under thear arms and
made them stay thear for quite awhile ountill they w pretty cold
then h let them come out and told them to leave his camp if ever
he caught them in his camp again he would tie a rock too thear
neck and throw them intoo the river

On November 13, 1862, Colonel Houk's battalion was ordered to Nashville, where it was to join the rest of the regiment under Major Cross,
reuniting the Third Tennessee for the first time in many weeks.

[December 11, 1862]
We was ordered to get readdey to take transpertation for Lew-
isville Ky and on December the 11th we loaded evrey thing a
steamboat and at 2 oclock we steamed out down the ohio river and
some time dureing the night our boat stuck it nose in too a sand
banke oposie Manshester whear we staid ountill about noon when
they finly got off

[December 14, 1862]

*on the 14 we landed at the warf in Cincinnatia ohio the Generel
had the longest gangplanke that they had run out and put a gard
on it with fixed Bayonet to keep all of us on the boat and late in
the day another boat pulled up alongside and made fast too our
boat we transferde all of our Belongins on too it then started on
down the river for Lewisville and we pulled up to the warf the
next day all went ashore we marched through Lewisville and
went intoo camp on the Lewisville and Nashville R R Isaac
Thompson my first cuson and Tom Scott come to sea us*

[December 16, 1862]

*on Sunday we tended preaching after which we got orders to
strike tentes we marched to the depo and loaded evrey thing on the
cars by 7 oclock. Started at 11 that night for Nashville Tenn past
through Bowlingreen Joust before reaching Mitchelville we come
to a tunel the rebels had dug and blasted a hole from the top of the
hill and filled it in so that trains couldent get through we ounloaded and went into camp the next day we started to march too
Nashville and after 2 dayes of hard marching we walked through
Nashville and camped on the franklin pike and that night I took
sick with the fever the next day the boyes carried me too the hospitel in an old deserted hous I lay thear on the floor for 12 days finley
old Doctor rodgers gave me out I was starveing for watter and he
wouldent let me have aney evrey time it shut my Eys I could see
the water runing over the gravels at home all he gave me was a
little brandy My Brother went and got a doctor from some ohio
reg he come and tooke charge of me let me have some water and I
began to mend from the start and was soon able to sit up when I
was able for dutey I returned to my Co found the reg in camp on
the Franklin pike and on Sunday night drawed 3 dayes rations
under marching orders on Sadurday we went too the creek and
washed our clothes on Monday we struck tentes and moved camp
about 2 hundred yardes*

[December 18, 1862]
*on the 18th we was ordered out at 12 oclock Drawed 3 dayes
rations readey to march at dailight stayed in camp all day*

[December 24, 1862]
*on the 24 we struck tentes and started for the Frunt ordered back
went intoo camp near the state prison*

[December 25, 1862]
*Brother John L. Haworth come over to sea us he belongs too the
2cd Tenn Cav being chismas day we tore down our tentes and
moved at about 30 yards put them up again*

[December 26, 1862]
*next day our reg went out gardeing a train hunting corn rained
all day we went out about 15 miles in the direction of Galitan got
back to camp about 11 oclock that night*

[December 27, 1862]
next day was Sunday rote a letter to Z. Morris 29 on gard dutey

[December 30, 1862]
*the 30th our reg was diging riful pites all day under Col Bird
brother John come and joined our Co on the 26 of Dec and has
been Sicke in the hospital ever since*

CHAPTER TWO
∼ 1863 ∼

[January 1863]
*In camp near Nashville Tenn called out at 8 oclock at night and
lay in the riful pites about one hour then was called out at 3 and
staid about an hour then again at dailight our Co was sent too
headquarters in the citey as gardes I had charge of the gardes at the
Zale Coffer hous*

On January 2, 1863, Brigadier General Spears took command of a brigade
composed of the First, Second, Third, Fourth, Fifth, and Sixth Tennessee Infantry. This was the First Brigade of Brigadier General J. S. Negley's Second Division. On the night of January 2 most of this brigade
escorted a wagon train from Nashville to the army at Murfreesboro and
was involved in the fighting there on January 3. The Third and Fifth Tennessee regiments were left behind in Nashville.

[January 3, 1863]
*On the 3 we was called out at 8 and stood in line of battle ountill
one Expecting to be attacked caled out again and lay in riful pites
ountill after dailight all of our Brigade gone to the frunt but the
3rd and 5th Tenn the hole reg on picket 2 1/2 miles west of Nashville I tooke breakfast the next morning at Mrs. Dunlapes.
Capt Wm C Haworth tooke sick I took command of the post
13 men one Corperel Captain Sawyers officer of the day went
through the state prison in charge of a squad of our boys the rest of
the day in camp nothing dooing.*

[January 8, 1863]

the 8th we was ordered on picket. we keep a chain gard around Nashville. Snowed hard all day and was varey cold I had the tooth ach all night. I had command of the middle post we was releived about 10 oclock and come to camp

[January 9, 1863]

and the next day being Sunday we had preaching. Lieut Baker preached his first sermon. he belonges to Co B 3ʳᵈ Tenn

[January 12, 1863]

on the morning of the 12 we was ordered out without rations Sargt Lewis and the Captins niger Cook brought out som rations late in the day

[January 13, 1863]

the next day we was ordered in off of picket at 3 oclock pm our reg was standing in line waiteing for us we fell in. Some got rations and some dident. we was gowing out forageing we struck some rebel cave 8 miles west of Nashvill and in the round we captured ^10^ prisners when ^we^ was gowing into camp.

[January 14, 1863]

the next morning we started earley and marched hard all day waded dog creek 5 times. Sometimes the creek was prettey deep. we camped in an open field in the mud never sleap aney ^that^ night. we joust had our overcoates it rained ountill about 4 oclock then commenced to sleat geteing colder all the time we started for camp at daylight 28 miles away a Blizerd come on from the North west with snow we had no rations. I slung my gun over my shoulder so that I could put my handes in my pockets we had no gloves we marched hard And it kept geting colder we had a rear gard to keep the ones up that gave out. my gun strap froze to my over coat. when in about a mile of camp I was so weake and tirred that I stoped and sit down. then I began to feal warm And I laid down. dident know aneything more ountill the rear gard 2 of them

was holding me up and trying to get me to camp they got thear
then the captain made some hot drinkes and put me in some hot
Blankes I got warmed up. In camp all day drying our clothes and
resting up that night drawed 3 dayes rations.

[January 15, 1863]
next morning Struck tentes and ready to march at daylight the
ground was coverd with ^snow^ and froze hard reported on the
Murfeburrow pike at 7 oclock our brigade in line we are garding
a wagon train of Amunition for Rosecrance at Stone River we
camped that night at Lavering

[January 16, 1863]
We started on at daylight reached Stone river joust before night
turned our train over too Rosecrance we crost Stone river marched
through Murfersburrow and went intoo camp about one mile out

[January 17, 1863]
the next day we was puteing up our tentes According to army
regulations and cut ditches around them then we was drilling
evrey day ountill Sunday when we had preaching by the regmen-
tal chaplin and that night I had the tooth ach awful bad never
sleap aney on Monday morning I went over to the 6th Tenn and
old Dr Moffin pulled my tooth then we was drilling evrey day
ountill the first of febuary.

[February 1863]
We garded a train out forageing come back about 9 oclock that
night rote a letter to Ant Sarah H. Dillion Georgetown Ills had
an oyster supper the next day I drilled our Co in the manuel of
arms our Co all on picket we have bin in the army 12 monthes
today Hamilton Bunch our teamster come in with his ankle
sprained the co come in off of picket at noon went out to drill
but it rained & we came in Next day washing in the fore noon
drawed Rations then skirmish drill Detaled 4 men 1 Sarg 2 cor-
perel for forage duty and 4 men to gard head quarters up at 3

*oclock starting out the detales I am actin ordey [orderly] Sargt me
and A.F. Northern went over too the 3rd Batalion pionier core
hospitel to see James N. Northern Got back at sundown all of the
co that is Able for dutey ordered on picket nex day at station No 2
chain gard. rained all day and nite. Captain Okeath officer of the
day releived the next day at 10 oclock by the 16th ohio and 19th
Ills. raining all morning Capt Sawyeras gone to Nashville the
next day in camp all day Still raining shot off our guns*

[February 19, 1863]

*Feb 19th called up at 2 oclock drawed 2 dayes Rations started with
the wagons forageing for corn we found some out 16 miles near
rover we had to fight Some rebel came while the boyes gather the
corn we Drawe them off Loaded our wagons and started back. at
dark come part of the way And went into camp for the rest of the
night next morning come to camp I give out and had to ride in
on one of the loaded wagons Generl Spears in command 3 trains
of cars at the Depo raining and thundering all day Varey cold 4 of
our Co vaxinated the Small Pox is in camp we are gardeing the
6 Tennessee Captin Sawyears Elixander Morgan John Fry and
Thomas Northern A. F. Northern was detaled on Speciel Duty by
orders of Generel Thomas too gow into East Tenn To burn and
destroy the R R Bridges East of Knoxville on the East Tenn and
Virginia R R*

    *On the 23, drilling W^m C Haworth in command of our co
Batalion Drill in the after noon prepareing for review the first
East ^Tenn^ Brigade composed of the following regmentes the
first second third fifth and sixth Tenn inft went on Review we
had a grand Display We got the prais fom the Generel Generl
Spears in command of our Brigade Genrel Negley commanding
the Division 14 the Army Core Center army of the Cumberland
five men detaled to gow forageing with three dayes rations Isaac
H Smith vaxinated W C Haworth sicke I driled our Companey
raining we elected 5 men from our Co too the roal of honer John
Tate John Maples Hamulton Bunch Thomas Faulkner and*

*Franklin Maples was Elected they are on Examination mustered
for pay Driling in the after noon*

[March 1863]
*Called out drawed 3 days rations started out forageing rode in the
wagones went about 24 miles. Captured 63 prisners came back
without aney forage got to camp about midnight plom wore out.
Sargt Lewis and all of the men that ^was^ not with us yesterday
was driling all day made a detale of 12 men and one Corperel
for picket Birt Hodges returned from Tenn I drilled our co in the
fore noon Batalion drill in the after noon by Col Wm Cross I rote
a letter to L J Ballinger Birt Hodges started back to east Tenn I
sent my letter By him He charges one doller for each letter the first
and second Tenn strucke tentes And marched in the direction of
Nashville Drawed 3 dayes rations Makeing out the payroles the
paymaster came to camp and paid us off I got $68^{00} took sick that
night Prettey sicke dident eat aney thing laying in my tent all day
12 men and one corperel for picket drawed rations.*

[March 11, 1863]
*11th 12 men one corpl for picket again geting Readdey for inspec-
tion Drilling most all of the time the men that was selected to
the Roal of honer was ordered to report at Headquarters Nathan
Milles Hamilton Bunch and Ben Bradshaw was selected Co drill
in fore noon Batalion drill in the after noon Cleaning up our
Arms for review 10 men 1 Corp for picket one Sargt for fatigue
duty Batalion drill fightting on our right wing Canonading
prettey heavey the next morning at dailight ordered out on quick
time with one section of the Second Ky batterry to Relieve the 5th
Tenn lay on our arms all night expecting to be attacted the 23rd we
was relieved by the 5 tenn and one Co of the first Wisconsin inft
Next day we was ordered out to support the picketes on double
quick time the Johneys never showed up we come too camp on the
25 I detaled one corperel and 10 men to ounload Cars at the Depo I
was in command our regment was on review raining the next day
all of our regment on picket our Co at Station No 2 Lieut Black*

*and Lieut Cross in Command skirmishing some out in the frunt.
Our Division on review the next day skirmishing prettey heavey
earley in the morning releaved by the 69th Ohio I went across
the creek too whear the 25 Ills was camped to sea the boys from
Georget^own^*

[March 28, 1863]
*28 cloudey and cold cleaning up our arms for inspection sunshine
after noon had Co Inspection then Co Drill Drawed axes and
hatchists then had skirmish drill.*

[April 1863]
*Captain Sawyers Alixander Morgan John W. Fry and A.F.
Northern come back from East Tenn wher they ^have^ bin on
speciel dutey East of Noxville Thomas S. Northern was left sick
in Knox Co Tenn Henrey Davis and Housten come too the Co
Drilling most all of the time. got a letter from home. drawed 3
dayes rations ordered to be readey to move Next morning struck
tentes Marched out at 11 oclock marched through Murefsbur-
row Marched out on the pike leading to Liberty Tenn marched
hard never stoped until 11 oclock that night got something too eat
and rested ountill one oclock when we was called intoo line and
Marched out Never stoped ountill Sunup went intoo camp and
got some breakfast we caught up with one Brigade and one battery Drove in the rebel picketes and the battle of liberty was on it
was pretty heavey while it lasted by 10 oclock we had drove the
rebels out of town capturing several prisners and a wagon train
canonading in the frunt our reg is garding the wagon train we
went intoo camp about one mile above liberty on the River hear
we turned in our tentes and drawed little shelter tents we call
them Dog Tentes*

Until this time most Civil War units were using large tents shaped somewhat like Indian teepees, each one large enough for perhaps a dozen men.
They had many disadvantages, one of which was size and bulk. It took

several wagons just to haul a unit's tents. Small shelter tents were issued in an effort to cut down the size of the army's trains (wagons). Each of the new tents would hold one or two men. World War II soldiers called them pup tents.

we was called out next morning at 3 oclock and started for Carthage Tenn Generl Stanlys Brigade of Cavelrry is Escorting us we past through Alixander the next day then the escort went back that night we camped on the cumberlin river oposit Carthage laying in camp resting ountill noon then we marched upon the hill stacked armes waiteing for the wagon train to be ferryed across the river Joust one small steamboat to take us all over we finly got across the river about 2 oclock that night marched out through Carthage about 2 ½ miles and went intoo camp on a Creeke.

that day I tooke the Co down and we all scalded and washed our cloathing after we come back we ditched around our tentes A wild deer ran through our camp a detale of 10 men and my Self as Sargt was sent out on picket. The rebel bush whackers fired on our post joust at daylight but we went after them and they got away we was reliived at 4 oclock p m by the 5th Tenn down washing Brigade drill from one to 3 oclock by Generel Spears the first time that he has ever drilled the brigade 11 men and 1 Lieut for picket dutey Co drill by ordley sargt Lewis Brigade drill in the after noon by Generel Spears and Col Joseph Coopper of the 6th Tenn Company inspection in the fore noon and resting after noon next my self and 10 men detaled for piket duty Lieut Ledgerwood in command of the station An alarm was raised about 4 oclock the next morning by a rebel trying to crawl up on our outpost releaved at 9 oclock by the 6th Tenn the 3rd Tenn was ordered to report at headquarters for Scout dutey the order was countermanded and the reg returned to camp Generel Crooks brigad past By our brigade was ordered out we marched South through Carthage and crost the Cumberlin river marched out South About 2 miles we could Sea some rebel Infantry we formed line of battle and lay down we staid thear ountill 12 oclock at night Then we

was ordered back too camp reached camp about 3 oclock muddey
cold and about wore out and a little mad.

[April 16, 1863]
*16th me and 9 men 1 corpel sent out on picket duty we are at sta-
tion no 2*

[April 17, 1863]
*next day releaved by the 6th Tenn we got our mail to day rote
a letter to Z Morris Co drill then brigade drill After noon by
Generel Spears and Colonel Coopper 4 of our Co in the gard hous
caught out last night too a dance*

[April 18, 1863]
*next day in camp all day raining our boys was releast Co drill by
Lieut Haworth brigade Drill by Spears Alixander Morgan and
Henrey Overbay was placed under Arest and made to dig up a
big tree for shooting at a dear that ran through our campes. It was
against orders to fire a gun in camp*

[April 22, 1863]
*22 one Sargt one corpl & 8 men for picket Co drill by me batalion
drill by Spears next day Co drill by Lieut Haworth*

[April 23, 1863]
*Brigade drill by Col Cooper the next day Generel Spears and
Col Shelby of the 5th Tenn was drilling us all day I took the sick
headach had it prettey bad all night the 25th 10 men one sargt for
picket I am sick yet the next 2 dayes we dident drill aney Cloudey
and rainey I rote some letters the next day was Sunday I am on
the sick list yet Had preaching in the morning no driling to Day
nor the next day. Captain Sawyers and my self was tendeing
a cort marshel whear Lee Davis and Husten Davis was being
^tride^. we were witnesses for the government.*

[April 30, 1863]

Last day of the Month ordered out on generel review Under Generel Crook and we was mustered for pay.

[May 1863]

Late lieut Mat H Peck come to visit us. He was elected first Lieutenant when our company was organized and in the face of the enemy he deserted his Co and showed cowerdice. he was then dishonorebly dismist from the servis of the United States by the ware department nobbody wanted to sea him he soon left. wash day 10 men one corpl for picket Drilling evrey day

[May 5, 1863]

On the 5 we was paid off I got $34⁰⁰ two monthes pay

[May 6, 1863]

the next day I took my Brother Ike to the hospitel that morning when we was geting breakfast Tom Nelson stabed Eb Simmons with his pocket knife ike is wors today

[May 7, 1863]

next day was wash day W S Troutman does my washing Batalion drill by Col Cross a fleat of 6 steam boates come up loaded with supplyes and ammunition Capt Sawyers and I went over to Carthage.

[May 11, 1863]

May 11th a spy was hung over by the river today he hand bin in our campe several days claimed he was visiting some relatives and that morning went to the general and got a pass too go home. Said he lived south across the river after he had started and was over the river he was reported and the generel started Cav after him the[y] caught him at the out side Cav Picketes and Brought him back Generl Crookes conveaned a drumhed Cort Martial to try him they had him to pull of his bootes and all of his clothing while they searching his clothes A Soldier who was lookeing over his bootes found one half sole fastened on with some screws He tooke his

*pocket knife and loosent them lifteing up the backe of the half
sole and found a compleate map of our fortes and whear evrey peas
of Artilrey was he was tride condemed and hung in side of 2 hours
I was thear*

[May 13, 1863]
*May 13 from that on to the last of May I was detaled for picket
dutey and drilling everey day it did20t rain I was haveing the
chilles evurey day and wouldent go too the hospitel ountill the 29
the boyes got a stretcher and carried ^me^ over too the hospitel.*

[June 2, 1863]
*Generl Review under Generel Crooks on the 2cd of June Generel
Crook with his command struck tentes and marched out crosing the
Cumberlan river gowing South*

[June 3, 1863]
*the next morning we struck tentes at 8 oclock A M we crost the
hill and camped whear the 92 ohio had bin camped I come over in
the ambulance Generel Crook is engageing the rebels we can hear
his artilrey no boates comeing up the river we have to forage for
rations. Capt Sawyers with all of our Co gardeing a wagon train
gowing after rations had little round with some rebel cavl*

[June 10, 1863]
*June 10th Col Stokes and the 6 Tenn gone over the river on a scout
raining all the next day I am not able for dutey yet I have had
the fever and it has gone too my feet I cant walk without help the
doctor has the boyes to carry me out to the big watering troft whear
the spring is and I sit for severel hours each day bathing my feet in
that spring water for severel hours when its fit weather.*

[June 12, 1863]
*On the twelf was in campes all day some better W C Haworth tooke
our Co as gard for a wagon train gowing to Galiton after supplies
He expret ninety dollars for me to B. Channaday Georgetown, Ills
they are to keep my money for me ountill I get out of the army*

[June 15, 1863]
on the fifteenth of June I drawed my gun and walked to town

[June 18, 1863]
on the 18 had Co drill. Col L C Houk come to sea us. Dean Lewis,
regmental Quarter Master come Reported for duty the male come
in the 11th Ky mounted inft come too us the rebels captured our
male and 15 men the regment orded up at 3 oclock and lay in the
rifel pites our pickets fired on acros the river we struck tentes and
moved over on the Galiton pike Camped on top of a high hill

[June 19, 1863]
Next morning called up at 3 oclock Lay in the rifel pites ountill
after sun up Blockade detale out our brigade surgen was captured
by Morgans men 152 of the 11th Ky mounted Inft went out on a
scout W.C. Haworth in command of the blockadeing detale 24 still
blockadeing geteing readey to fight John Morgan next day. W.C.
Haworth was sick not able for dutey Up at 3 evrey morning in the
workes ready. John A Fisher left for Nashville Heney Collins died
I took 6 men and dug his grave And at 3 oclock we berried Collins
with Military honors

[June 30, 1863]
on the 30th Daniel T S Garvins Died in the hospital.

[July 1863]
July out in the rifel pites at 10 oclock struck tentes and moved off of
the hill we Berried Garvins I drilled our Co in the fore noon then
we had an Election too Elect a delegate to our National Conven-
tion we Elected Joseph Gilbreath of Jefferson County East Tenn
makeing out our pay roles the male came in B Canady got the
$90⁰⁰ I sent them a fleat of 5 steam boates come up from Nashville
A F Lewis come up on them 6 men detaled to ounload boates me
and 12 men 2 corperel for picket Lieut Ledgerwood in command
the station on the Galiton pike releived by the 6 Tenn the Steam

boates left at dalight returning to Nashville Co inspecion at 4
oclock

  9 men and 3 corperel for picket duty. Capt Sawyers officer of
the day. John W. Fry was detaled as our Carpenter.

[July 12, 1863]
on the 12 we hear that Generel Grant has captured Vicksburge
thundering and raining all night 3 men for fatigue Dutey Bilde-
ing a pontoon Bridge Across the Cumberlan river. The male came
in after Night. Co drill I am not able to go on the Drill yet. Me
and A. F. Lewis went to town. I went on picket with 10 men
and 3 corperl the 5th Tenn went out on a Scout across the river. I
detaled 9 of our Co to go with them.

[July 13, 1863]
The next morning a rebel was crawling up on my out post he
couldn't fool Ben Yates. he shot him he got away but we found
blood on the leaves the next day. Our scouts come in. A fleat of
steam boates come up Loaded with rations and amunition that
is two things that we have too have to carry on a war me and
Elmore Edmons down in town all day.

[July 26, 1863]
on too the 26 it was detales for picket every day 26th ^50^ of our
reg went out on a scout on the gun boat landed after dark oposit
Hartsville we had a citicen gide we sliped through the woodes and
about one oclock at night we quitley Surrounded Col Loves hous
and captured 3 rebel officers. we staid around thear ountill after
diner then we started to march to camp gathered up severel horses
we met a bunch of our Caverly that had gone down to help us out
if we got too many rebels engaged we camped about midnight

[July 27, 1863]
We all marched out early struck the Midelton turn pike about
10 oclock our command went up the pike And the cav went by
Lebanon

[July 28, 1863]
They come into camp about one o'clock next Day with 7 prisners
pickets come in raining 20 men started out on a scout at 2 oclock at
night Captin Sawyears in command

[July 29, 1863]
the next day was wash day the male come in we got word that
John Morgan had bin captured in ohio

[August 1863]
We had generl inspection and we was paid off and settled with
the government for clothing. I had 15ᵗʰˢ comeing to me I drawed 4
monthes pay $54⁰⁰ me and John Fry bought us a 32 caliber Smith
and Weston pistel guns $26⁰⁰ Each [unintelligible] throwed in
raining Drilling in the fore noon by W C Haworth Batilion and
skirmish drill after noon by Col Cross

[August 8, 1863]
On the 8ᵗʰ the rebels attacted our outpost wounded one man and
drove ^them^ into our picket line thear we stoped them and drove
them back. Jasper P. Buckelew received his commission as first
Lieut of our co Wᵐ M Sawyers promoted to Lieut Col of reg Wᵐ C
Haworth promoted to Captain of Co K Sargt Wᵐ M Lewis gone
on a secret mission intoo East Tenn 10 men 2 corperel for picket Co
inspection drawed hates turned in our gunes drawed some with
Bayoneets 14 men 1 Sargt 1 Lieut for scout duty made out an ordi-
nance report I am in command of our Co the scout come in most of
our boys went to town to hear Col Stoakes speak

[August 9, 1863]
Col Sawyers come in next day 9 men 2 corperel one Sargt for
picket I went 3 men to go on a Scout
I was in charge of 9 men loadeing the wagons with 9 days sup-
plie. Struck tentes Started crosing the river took us all night to get
every thing over Col Sawyers in command of the reg 21 marched
through Middleton Col Stokes in command of our brigade one
man one corperel for picket 22 marched through Elixander camped

one mile above 6 men to go forageing 6 men one Sargt to gard the
wagon train to Carthage after rations

[August 24, 1863]
I went on the 24 we was loading the wagons all day. Captain
Slover in command I have 14 men on picket all day and night we
captured 9 prisners I [unintelligible] a wagon so we could all ride
back to camp then I turned the prisners over to Col Mansford I
had R.I. Morgan our sutter to order me a Jackit from Cincinnat-
tie Me and 8 men 1 Corperel for picket. Me and John Tate got a
pass and went out side of the pickets on returning the Command
was under marching orders the wagon train was sent back to
Carthage too ounlod drawed 6 dayes rations and marched out
at 12 oclock for McMinville Tenn went into camp that night at
Liberty called up at 3 oclock marched out at 6. marched 21 miles
the roades was varey dusty waded Westerfalls creek and went into
camp on the creek

[September 11, 1863]
Called up again at 3 oclock marched out withe the fife and drum
making music Marched through McMinnville and went into
camp whear the 86 Indianna had bin camped I was ordered to
take 18 men and 1 corperel and go on picket I have charge of sta-
tion no 6 down by the woolin mills

[September 12, 1863]
Relieved the next day by the rest of our co the troopes that was
camped hear have all gone to the frunt 17 men one Lieut and 1
Sargt detailed for picket

[September 13, 1863]
The next day me with 9 men one corperel went on picket at Sta-
tion 5. Captin Roberts in command I was up ountill after one
oclock Sund 8 men one Sargt one Corpere made 2 reliefs of our
*Co the 5th Iowa and the first Middle Tenn Batterry come ^in^*
also the 5th Tenn Inft come in Genarel Spears in Command he

marched them so hard that 2 men was killed with heat

[September 14, 1863]
Me and Wm Haines and Elic Morgan got a pass and went to town never got back ountill after rool call one man detaled to load rations orders to be readey in the morning

[September 15, 1863]
Broke camp at 6 oclock marched all day Varey dustey Camped on top of Cumberlan Mountain at a little Sumer town called Busabeys Springes

[September 16, 1863]
Marched out at daylight Dust is terable Camped on the mountain no water except a little we got out of a pond

[September 17, 1863]
Broke camp at daylight and marched hard come off of the mountain intoo Sequochie Valley and found plentey of water I gave out and went to the wagon and it broke down I got 2 wagon wheals from a farmers wagon and come intoo camp after dark we ar camped 11 miles Above Jasper Tenn We are out of rations

[September 18, 1863]
Moved out the next morning at daylight our Co is the rear guard past through Jasper camped half mile below the wagons all gone to Bridgeport for supplies detaled 6 men from our Co to go as gardes Nothing to eat hear Me and Wm Haines went out side of our lines to A farm hous and got a good diner 7 men one corperl for picket ordered to camp about noon.

[September 19, 1863]
Struck tentes and Marched to the mouth of Battle Creek whear we camped the pioniers are puteing a pontoon Bridge Across the Tenn River finished it on the 19th the train come up and we drawed rations then all crost the river and started fur the frunt

The battle of Chickamauga was about to begin, but the Third Tennessee
was too far away to become involved, a stroke of good luck for them since
it turned out to be one of the bloodiest battles of the war. Because of a
tragic mistake in Union command the federal forces were routed and were
fleeing into Chattanooga from one direction as the Third Tennessee was
coming in from the other direction.

> [September 20, 1863]
> *Marched into Chattanooga about 3 p m pretty heavey fighting
> gowing on out South order to Join Generl Tomas at the frunt we
> started out About dark diden't get thear ountill the order w coun-
> termanded and we was put on picket*
>
> [September 21, 1863]
> *The next day it was mostly artilerry fightting Joust at night we
> ^was^ ordered out on a fors march to support Generel Thomas
> who was hard prest near Crawfish Springes we moved in and
> took position on Thomases right and piled up loges and rockes for
> protection it wasent long ountill Longstreats Core made a charge
> but we dident let them pass Tomas was holding the rebel army
> back while Rosencrants was moveing the rest of the army in side
> of the fortification. and he helt them.*

General George Thomas saved the Union army from total defeat, and the
men of the Third Tennessee could claim the honor of being a part of that
action. The Union forces were very close to losing Chattanooga.

> [September 22, 1863]
> *Jous before daylight Thomas quitley moved out and went in side
> of the works our reg went up the wagon road south of Chatta-
> nooga to the top of lookout Mountain and took a position across
> the mountain joust South of the big Hotel to gard the signel Core
> we cut down trees and piled up loges and rockes to gard Against
> Cav*

[September 23, 1863]

the next day was Sunday Not much fighting today we havent had Aney thing to eat since yesterday morning after dark the Captins darkey cook sliped through and brought a little provision Generl Whealers cav brigade has bin trying to drive us off Joust before dark a rebel officer come rideing up the road with a white flag we ceaste firing he rode up and called for the officer in command Col Cross steped out and told him that he commanded that reg the rebel officer ^said^ he was instructed to give him Generel Whealers compliments And demand his ounconditional surrender Co Cross straitent up stept out a little closter and Said give Generl Wheler my complimentes and tell him this is the 3ʳᵈ Tenn and dont no what Surrender means if he wantes us to come and get us. The officer hesitated about moveing Col Cross ses you can retire and he turned his hors and started back lowering his whit flag the Col told him he had better keep his flag up ountill he got out of reach of our gunes it wasent long ountill the fight opened up good and hot but they never broke our lines about 2 o'clock they ceased fireing and one of our officers craled along down the line and whispered to us to fall back quietley and meat at the sumer hotel we tooke the signel core boys with us. we had 2 boyes with us that had bin raised near thear and new whear we could get off of the mountain on the N W corner. we slide down and under cover of the fog we sliped along up the R R and got into Chattanoga and joined our army at dailight

That army was now besieged in Chattanooga. For the next few weeks it would come close to starving, subsisting on what supplies could be hauled by wagon from Bridgeport, Alabama, over sixty miles of primitive road under the guns of Confederate raiders. The Third Tennessee was lucky once again. They were sent out of Chattanooga to help guard the vital supply line and apparently escaped the worst of the suffering endured by the troops left behind.

[October 1863]
About the first of the month our Co moved up the Tenn river on
the North side. Went into camp at the mouth of Saddey Creek on
the Tenn river. I took 10 men and went to gard a wagon train
to Bridgeport Alabama after supplies. Comeing back I rode with
negrow Jim he was driving the sutlers wagon he complained
of being sick. when we got to camp the doctor said Jim had the
Smallpox and so the Col put all of us that was with the train
about a mile back in the timber and put a gard around us and we
staid thear until all had the smallpox who would take it I never
got it about the last of Nov. we burnt up everything hous bedeing
Evrey except our clothing that we washed and scalded good then
we joined our reg on Sunday the 29th

[November 30, 1863]
the paymaster come down to pay off our command on Monday
we was paid off I got $68^{00} 4 monthes pay the next day me and
Elmore Edmons went up on Sale Creek to sea some girls we staid
all night and our Co left camp that night

Once Chattanooga was secured, the next problem for the Union commanders was Knoxville. Confederate General Longstreet's Corps had been sent east before the battle at Missionary Ridge, and on November 29 he attacked Knoxville. Although the attack failed, there was fear that he might be planning another attack or an invasion of East Tennessee. The Third Tennessee was in the midst of a fast movement to block Longstreet.

[December 2, 1863]
Comeing back next morning we stoped at John Emerrys and got
Breakfast then come to camp gathered up our out fits and started
to Kingston whear our tropes are gowing too. that night we staid
all night with widdow Hixes.

[December 3, 1863]

Started out early next morning walked hard all day And before night we caught up with the wagon train we camped that night on Whites Creek me and Price and went out and staid all night with a man by the name of Johnson the girls played and Sang for us

[December 4, 1863]

The next night we got too Kingston about darke we staid with the paymaster

[December 5, 1863]

Next day we walked steadey all day caught up with the 5th Tenn Inf and a Baterry we finally found our reg in Camp oposit Londen on the Tenn River the rebels had burnt out the Center of the long R R Bridge crosing the Tenn River. Then they coupled and Engin with steam up too a long train of cars the engineer turned on the steam then jumped off and they all went intoo the Tenn river we could sea the cars piled up above the water we drawed Rations varey cold we captured 6 peases of Artilerry. they was all spiked

[December 7, 1863]

On Sunday we was ordered to put up our tentes. Alix Morgan got leave from Col Cross too go home to recruit got orders to be ready too march in the morning for Knoxville

[December 8, 1863]

moved out on the road and lay thear ountill 10 oclock Burnt up 2 houses to warm by camped that night 13 miles below Knoxville

[December 9, 1863]

on the Ninth we marched out early I went on ahead stoped at a hous and got breakfast the captin is sicke he come up in the ambulance. we marched through Knoxville about 3 oclock thear was souch a crowd out to sea us that we could hardly get by we camp

*up about 2 miles too the old fare groundes and camped I took a
gard and went over too the 9th Tenn cav and brought Huston
Kates a deserter from our Co and put him in the gard house.*

[December 10, 1863]
*Next morning our command was moving up to Strawberry
plains when we come to the Guse valley road we went on that
and started for our homes we hirred a man with a wagon too haul
our knapsackes and gunes and Capt W C Haworth ^was sick^
we crost Holsten river at Nances ferry let the wagon go back from
thear got home before sundown the first time we have bin home
since joining the army we joust staid one night*

[December 11, 1863]
Joined our reg at Strawberry plains the next day

[December 12–13, 1863]
*we rested up the next day then marched up on the north side of
Holstean river and went into camp, on Richland near the old
Baptist church*

[December 14, 1863]
*the next day a portion of Longstreates troops attacted us we
formed line of battle and moved out and we skirmished with
them ountill our battery got in position then Generel Spears give
the command to fix Bayonetes and charge and we soon had them
moveing. we come varey near geting thear artilerry. we moved
on after them evrey time that they would find a good place they
would stop and show fight we kept that up ountill we had drove
them back beyond the mouth of Bufalow*

CHAPTER THREE
~ 1864 ~

[January 1, 1864]

And thear we went into camp in a fine grove of oak timber east of the big Mile belonging too Ant Polley Gilmore and was in camp thear on the night of the first of January which was the coldest night ever known thear the river froze over solid kept us cutting down trees and bildeing fires all night never slept aney we staid thear for over a weak then we broke camp and marched Back to the north side of the river oposit the R.R. Bridge at Strawberry plains And dug riful pits and a lot of rails on the center of the R.R. Bridge [space] Longstreet Armey was moveing back down the River we had a barrel of cole oil pored over thoes railes and the next day we fired them and lay in our rifel pites and Kept the Johneys off of the bridge ountill the middle span was burnt out then our army moved back sloley In line of battle and we made a stand evrey time we had a good position they finley stoped and our brigade went into camp at armstrongs ford on the Tenn River 3 miles above Knoxville.

Despite Grant's urging, the Union commanders decided against offensive operations because of the cold weather and lack of food and forage. The soldiers were in sad condition. When Major General John Schofield arrived at Knoxville to take command, he found the Twenty-Third Corps reduced to only three thousand men. All had been living on half rations for some time. Most were poorly clothed, and some had no shoes. Thousands of dead horses and mules littered the streets. Shortly after Schofield's arrival the railroad to Chattanooga was opened. But Grant continued to worry about Longstreet. He had no good intelligence about the Confederate forces or their intentions. Something had to be done.

[February 3, 1864]

*Feb 3rd we was in camp at Armsstronges Ford 3 mile above
Knoxville on the Tenn River I had gone out on picket with part
of our Company. The captin sent word for me to report at his
tent and when I reported I found our Col and General Crook the
commander of our Army at Knoxville General Crook motioned
me to a seat clost by him he told ^ me^ that he was fearful that
Longstreat had bin reinfosed by troopes from General Lee, Longstreates headquarters was then in New market. he said he wanted
a man to gow into his camp and get that Infurmation and that
they had decided that I was the one to go He Said Will you go I
told him I wasent kean for the Job but if I was detaled Ide go.
He[unintelligible] put his hand on my shoulder and said Sargt
get ready and report at my Headquarters at one oclock and I could
select a man to go with ^me^. It was then ten oclock. I selected
Mark Price because he new ^the^ country that we had to travel
through. we got some diner and each one was provided with a
rebel jacket and at one oclock we reported at Generl Crookes tent
he give us full instructions and we left Evrey thing that might
identifie us if we was captured he sent one of his officers with us
and he past us through the outside cavelry picketes then we traveled through the woddes we had about 20 miles to go and when
dark come we was getting clost too richland ^creek^. we sliped
in the back way to Mrs. Prices Mark's mothers to find out about
the rebel scoutes then we hurried on Comeing too the crossing on
Richland we went and called up old man Stone He told us that
a forageing party of rebels had come in about dark and camped
at the fure end of the bridge and our only chance to cross was the
bridge or wade the creek. It was an old fashined Bridged weather
borded And covered we decided to try the Bridge first I told Mark
to have his revolver In his hand ready and if thear was aney one
on picket they would halt us then we was both to shoot at him and
run Back and if we got seperated we was to meet at the south east
of the old Baptist church then we would wade the creek we walked
right through we had our Rebel unaform on the wagons was
parked on the left side of the road and the gardes were sleaping on*

the other side one soldier raised up rubeing his Eyes and looked
at us but never said aney thing we steped along pretty livley and
from that on we traveled in the road abouut Midnight we got to
Larner Bradshawes he lived on the west side of Holstean River
opposit too whear my father lived and whear I was raised he was
a strong friend of our Side we called him up and the girles got up
and [?]some supper he lived in a log hous and some of the chinking
was out and Aron Kiles that Southern man lived up on the bluff
I had arrested him and sent him to Knoxvill for violating his
oath by giveing information to the Rebels 2 of his girles was up
and saw the light and sliped down and saw me through the cracks
and as son as daylight came the[y] crost the river went to General
Perryes quarters and told him about us so he sent a captin and
about 20 men over to capture us I made arrangement with the old
man Bradshaw to go intoo the rebel campes the next day selling
cakes and pyes and to get the information that I wanted and just
at daylight we ^took^ a quilt apeas and went up near the top of
[rich?] hill in a thicket. Some of them was to bring us something
to eat and some water we roled up and went to sleap and sleap
nearly all day. we waited ountill It was geting darke we decided
to gow Down and sea what the trouble was. Theas rebels had
bin searching evrey whear all afternoon Kept all the family in
the hous so they couldent get us word and then they formed a line
around the hous and all lay down and waited and we walked
in to the trap the first I new they sprang up all Around us with
thear guns at aready saying surrender or we will Kill you I looked
back and saw they was all around us so we had to surrender they
took us up by Kiles and the 2 girls who had reported on us came
out and joust shouted So glad that they helped to get us captured
then we crost the river in a canoo they stopped at my fathers and
Mother begged for the captin to let me stay all night And him and
ten men staid that night Mother sliped me a hundred Dollers in
Confederate Money Said it might help me to get away the nexte
morning Mother and Julyann went with us we was taken before
General Perry He was a blusterry high strung old man He ques-
tioned me a good deal and curst and Abused me because I lived

*in the South and was fightting in the Armey of Lincons Hire-
lings and Nigers he said longstreat was away but as Soon as he
returned he would Convean a drumhead cortmarshel and they
would fix me We was taken to old log hous whear Gabriel Morgan
famley lived It was used as the Brigade guard house. Old Perrey
told the captin ^to^ keep clost watch on me the next day Marey
Haworth my brother's wife Julyann Williams Manday Haworth
and Kate Kersey came over to sea me and they pursuaided the
lieutenant in charge to take us over joust acros the field ^to^ take
supper at Mary Haworths. He took us over with 4 gardes staid
untill 9 oclock the next day Mary and Julyan was over and the
lieut agreed to take us over that night to stay all night about Dark
we went over the lieut and me was talking we was a little behind
the rest he said he felt sorry for ^me^ that longstreat had returned
and ^he^ had orders to take me before a Drumhead court martial
the next morning at eight o'clock at Longstreates head quarters in
New market. I had aranged with one of the gardes to give me a
chance when we went out. I was to give him the hundred dollers
of confederate money and he was to shoot over my head when I
ran but that dident work we hadent been thear long ountill he
was sent back and another guard come in his place. That night the
Lieut told Mary they would like to have Breakfast early so they
got up early. I lay on the floor in frunt of the fire place dident sleap
much. 2 soldiers on guard all the time. When I got up and washed
and buttoned up my Rebel Jacket I had made up my mind that I
was gowing to get away. The oold Morgan House was a doubble
log hous with entry between and Elic Morgan had built a too
story frame house west of the north end of the old hous and had a
big fire place in the west end. bed on each Side and the table set
back a little*

Throughout this passage, which David transcribed after his return home,
he reveals details that he could not have known until well after the events
he describes here.

8 of the guards I and Price and the Lieutenant sit down to Eat Breakfast. I took a sup of coffee pushed back my char gaging said I was sick the water bucket sit on a shelf joust out side of the dore next too the old hous on the west side As I past the bed I just slid my cap off kept it down kept my other hand on my stomach and bending over like I was gowing to throw up. I asked Julyann to give me a drink of water. She opened the door and Handed me some water I took a Sup and looked around to sea if the 2 gardes had thear gunes in thear hands They was leaning against the jam when July ann took the diper She whispered too gow pulled the door further open and I joust sailed out. hit the ground runing She Slammed the door to turned and locked it then stood with hear back against the door ountil they jerked her loos. When they sean that I was gone they all made a rush at once Some falling over the chairs then when they finley got out of the hous they run around to the left and I went out west through a young orchard at the back side of the orchard was a rail fence. I joust put my hands on the top Rale and leaped over, then I started north They never got site of me after I went out of the house. never shot at me I nearley flew ountil I got into the timber. it was about 2 miles too Loss Creek Sholes and I Ran all the way I past on the east side of our field could see the smoke comeing out of the chimbley but I knew it wouldn't doo to go thear. when I was gowing down the hill too the river I was in plain view of Mahlon Haworth He had 2 rebel gardes they happened to see me and they Ran into the hous and got thear gunes and tride to cut me off from the river but I speeded up and beat them As I went down the Bank I was pretty warm sweat running down my face I puled off my jacket tide it over one sholder and under the other arm. Kept running ountil the water was up too my waist It was awful cold mush ice on the water. When I got to whear I had to swim it liked to nocked the wind all out of me. I was afraid I would take the cramps being so warm and drown but I knew it was death behind me and I would take the chance when I felt bottom on the other side I hurried out ountide [untied] my jacket and put it on before I got up the bank it rattled was froze. I had about ¼ up hill through An corn field I

*soon warmed up I travled hard all day. They put a lot of cavelry
in small squades rideing the roades watching for me. I had to cross
the mane roades whear thear was timber on both side. I coulden
go in a field. I had no armes. I cut me a young Hickrey club. Joust
after dark I come too Mrs. Prices and old Harry was siting in
his cabin I caled too him he come out I saw 2 horses tied up at the
big hous. It was two rebel officers stoped thear for supper I told
Harry I would take the best hors cut the other one loos and ride
out I was tirred of walking. he said that wouldent doo Inman
had gone down the road with his Co I would be sure to run intoo
him I told Harry that I wanted to get too Wm Reedes over on flat
Creek Had to stay out of the road most of the time Harrey went
with ^me^ untill we got in About ¼ Reedes then he went back
and I started on down the old road and hadent ^gone^ far Intill
4 rebel Soldiers with thear gunes got up And I thought I had run
onto a picket Post. I never spok [?] did they could sea that I had
the rebel unaform finley they started to walk off and to the left
And I walked too the right I dident have any thing to say. I past
them and trotted on down the road to whear price lived It was
a log hous the door was fastened with a chain around the facen
and through the dore all was dark inside. we stoped hear as we
come up for Information. I called to price and his wife answered.
I asked her whear Mr. price was. Said She Dident know and told
^me^ to leave thear. I told her that I was Haworth no She said
the rebels Had shot Haworth the day befor for a spy at New Market No I told how I had mad my Escape and swam Holsten river
and now I was plum wore out and had to have help to get to my
armey She again told me to leave I then asked her if She wouldent
no my cap I wore a nice blew cap I told ^her^ to get up and Ide
hand my cap in through a crack She took it went too the fire place
stired up the coles then came back and ounfastened the door And I
steped in Side and Looked back at the bed thear sat Wm Reed with
a pistol in his hand I told him that I had joust past 4 rebel soldiers
up on the hill. I always have through that they was deserters trying to get to our army But they was afraid of my uniform read got
intoo his clothes pretty quicke and got out She was chaining up*

the doore as soon as we got out we crost Flat Creek and traveled through the woodes and about midnight we got too Leg Station. His mother in law lived thear. I joust had to rest had eat nothing since the night before Swam the river and had traveled hard all day read called her up and we went in I told her not to make any light they pulled off my jacket and Shoes an old grandma put her nightcap on me put me in her bed. I told ^them^ let me sleap 4 hours then we could make It in to our lines by daylight when they waked me up they had some hot coffey And a good supper I have always felt So thankful four such loyal old wiman as she was She was the good Samartan to me

We traveled on keeping away from the road and joust as it was getting daylight we come too the ridge whear our picketes was stationed when I left I told reed to wait thear ountill I called him I went along whisteling and calling for them not to shoot they let me get up pretty clost then the picket sang out halt he told ^me^ not to move ontill he called the reserve. The Lieutenant In Command Soon come then I was ordered to advance when I got too them I called back to Reed to come in the Lieut let us go on into camp I walked up to our Company joust as they was ready to eat Breakfast they all jumped up yelling So glad to sea me Back the Captin & Col Cross all came down. I told them I would like to eat some the first thing hadent Eat but one time in 2 nightes and one day. my brother took us up to his tent and we had Breakfast. They had got the word that I bin Cortmarsheld and Shot. As soon as we was through with Breakfast the Col come down. him and my brother and me went too General Crookes headquarters. he was glad to sea me. I made my report. I had got all the infermation that he wanted. Longstreat had not bin reinfost and thear was no Danger of him driveing our army inside of the fortifycations while in the rebel camp I noticed that Generl Perrys Brigade didn't have any bayonets They was in the charge on Fort Sanders whear our men slaughtered them with hand grenades and they throwed their bayonets away said they would not charge any more I was thear with General Crook ountill nearly noon give him full account of all of Longstreetes troopes and whear they were stationed at he told me he would give me a furlow for thirty days asked whear I wanted to go too.

I told him I would go back too Georgetown Illinois he shook handes with me again and thanked me for what I had ^done^ and to go to camp and rest up he told the captin not to put me on aney detals And when I got ready to start to come back and he would have my furlow made out.

David's information was crucial to the Union commanders. Contrary to their fears, Longstreet's twenty-thousand-man army had dwindled to about twelve thousand, all of whom were cold, hungry, and discontented. At least for the moment Longstreet had ceased to be a threat.

David added the following information to his transcription after the war.

The morning that I made my escape the first my folks new of it when part of the gardes come In told my father they wanted to search the hous he told them all right They searched every hole and throwed the feather bedes off and looked under Every one. one of ^them^ even looked up the chimey. Father said you don't think he would be up there do you he said G. D. yankeys could get aney whear they searched all the timber and thickets around clost when they heard that I crost the river they had some cavalry over thear. They patroled the roades watching for me to cross them. Late that day I come too the Stage road leading from Knoxville to Blains Cross Roades I had selected a place to cross it whear it was timber But our army had bin camped thear and they cut off all the small timber and thear the road was in a croked hollow when I got too the road I stoped to listen I heard the clank of Caverly sabreys and horses. I new what it was on the other side of the road was a little field and I couldent run over the ridge before they come round the turn I saw a big Bolder whear the leaves had piled up on the back side of it. I ran to it. Scratched out the leaves lay down And pulled them up over me the best that I could. They rode on by. I heard one fellow say if they caught me they wouldn't bother about takeing me back. As soon as every thing got still I made good time getting over and intoo the timber again.

M.F. Price come into camp 3 dayes after I did they put him on the train with a lot of other prisners and started him too Libey Prison he smashed the glass in the care window jumped through and got away from them Longstreat had the Lieutenants Commision Revoked put ^him^ in the rankes as a common Soldier that was in charge when I Escaped He deserted and made his way back intoo Indiana and in about three months after that Mother got a letter from ^him^ telling what they had don he was so anxious too now if I ever lived to get back to my companey. She answered him and told him after that thear being 4 of us boys in the Union army the rebels drove my father out of the State And they went to Georgetown [Illinois]and staied ountill after the war was over then I went thear and Brought them and the Captins widow and little girl Matildey back home on Halsten river.

My brother W.C. Haworth was captin of our Co. He had his wife and little girl brought down to campes then I got my furlow and we started from Knoxville too go to Georgetown Ills on the 22cd day of Febuary and we got to Gorgetown on the 29 took us 7 days and nightes to make the trip Marey and little girl went to live with my ant Sarah Dillon I spent the 30 days very plesantley they would make big diners then I would be called on too tell all about my capture and escape I told it ountill I got tirred of telling it I was the first soldier that come back thear after being captured the rebels captured 5 of our Co after we went up in East Tenn but never got but one of them into priso. Some way they couldn't hold us Tenn soldiers varey long we didn't like the crowd.

While David enjoyed his Illinois furlough, there were major changes being made in the leadership of the army. On February 28, President Lincoln named Ulysses S. Grant commander of all Union forces and gave him the rank of lieutenant general, the first officer to hold the rank since George Washington. Grant turned over command of the Western army to William Tecumseh Sherman.

> *March the 15 started to return to my reg the rodes were so muddy had to ^go^ to Danvil hors back. I had a doze photographs taken. Got a train out about Midnight got to Indianapolis at day light got a train out at 9 oclock A M got to Louisville Ky at 5 p m Staid all night got a train out the next morning run into Nashville at 5 p m went out and staid all night with Lieutenent Thomas S. Northern of Co B 9th Tenn Cavelrey*

While David slept in Nashville, Generals Grant and Sherman were meeting in another part of that town, starting to develop a common strategy for fighting the war. Grant was to advance against Lee at Richmond while Sherman was to move against Atlanta. There was to be no letup in the offensive until the Confederacy was destroyed. It was a decision that was to have fateful consequences for the Third Tennessee Regiment and the Haworth brothers.

> [March 18, 1864]
> *The next day at 4 p m started for Chattanooga run intoo a snow storm. Blockaded and stoped the train got to Chattanooga at 3 oclock on the 19. Staid all night. Left thear the morning of the 20th at 9 oclock changed cars at lovden at 5 run into Knoxville at 7 staid all night into morning of the 21 got a train for Mossey Creek whear my reg is me and James Yates got off at the waterstation went over by our old home I staid around thear resting and visiting 4 days my brother came along.*

At the end of March, Sherman was traveling through Tennessee, meeting with the major commanders of the force he was to lead into Georgia. In Knoxville that was Major General John Schofield. Schofield was the youngest of Sherman's army commanders and the least experienced. He had been in only one battle, at Wilson's Creek near Springfield, Missouri, which was a Union defeat. But Schofield was intelligent and ambitious and determined to use this opportunity to make a name for himself.

> [March 25]
> *We went up to Mossy Creek and found our regment. The next
> day our Company was ordered to Flatt Creek to garde the R.R.
> Bridge. Staid thear 2 days. got orders to be ready to march the next
> morning. Our division come in and the Ballence of our reg. We are
> under orders to gow to Georga to join Generel Shermans Army.*

The men of the Third Tennessee were now ready to move out. They were
probably carrying the minimum for survival. It would have included a
rifle, cartridge box, cap pouch, canteen, haversack, one wool blanket, and
a "gum" blanket, a rubberized sheet that could be used as a ground cloth
or poncho. In addition there was a bayonet, sometimes a hatchet, and a
skillet or some similar utensil for cooking. They probably carried very
little, if any, extra clothing. As veteran troops, the Tennesseans knew the
value of traveling light. That fit right in with Sherman's philosophy for
this campaign. He knew he was heading into a mountainous area that
would have very few roads. A long wagon train would bog down the
whole army. The men would carry on their backs enough to eliminate
three hundred wagons for each corps.

> [April 5, 1864]
> *On the morning of the fifth we marched out at daylight marched
> hard. Stoped and rested 2 ^hours^ in an open field one mile above
> Knoxville. Varey hot we then marched through Knoxville in plat-
> toon formation the streetes was joust packed with people to sea us
> maby for the last time with maney of our Boys ^one mile^ below
> we stoped on a creek and drawed 3 days rations after marching 4
> mile further we camped Set in raining me and James Yates went
> too a hous to sleap. Marched out on posse march at daylight the
> roads are varey Muddy I gave out with 6 others of my Co we
> caught up with our reg about 9 oclock that night near Lovden.*

Sherman was waiting for word that Grant had started his drive on Lee, waiting to coordinate his attack as they had agreed months before. On May 6 word came and Sherman gave the order.

One writer described the scene:

Two hundred and fifty-four cannon began to rumble, the barrier went up on 98,000 men, most of them between the ages of eighteen and twenty-five. They marched through wildflowers and fruit trees in bloom. Bees hummed. As the One Hundred and Fiftieth New York marched past the battlefield of Chickamauga, Private Charles E. Benton saw trees dead from bullet wounds, human skeletons working their way out of shallow graves. He saw "hands sticking up, dried skin to bones and weathered to the color of granite—fingers curved as if beckoning—one with index finger pointing upward." Thrushes sang, humming birds tossed among blossoms. It was May.[13]

[May 6]
We marched 25 miles today Evrey day was like this on ountill we got into Georga on the 10th we struck some rebel troopes near Dalton but soon drove them off

Sherman was moving south with 110,000 men organized in three columns: the Army of the Cumberland under Major General George Thomas, the Army of the Tennessee under Major General James McPherson, and the Army of the Ohio under Major General John Schofield. Schofield's force was the smallest of Sherman's armies with only 13,500 men, including some cavalry and twenty-eight artillery pieces. Its major component was the Twenty-Third Corps, and among its infantry units was the Third Tennessee. Sherman was determined to move fast and light. He ordered all personal equipment sent to the rear; only absolute essentials were kept. Each regiment was restricted to one wagon and one ambulance. He also severely restricted news reporters, with the result that very little news of his operations was printed in the northern papers.

After several days of marching and limited fighting, Sherman found himself blocked by Rocky Face Ridge, an obstacle that would have been difficult in the best of circumstances but was now heavily fortified by Confederate General Joe Johnston's troops. Studying his maps of the area, Sherman found a solution. There was a way around Rocky Face through Snake Creek Gap, a route the Confederates had somehow neglected to fortify. He moved most of his force into position as though he intended to attack Rocky Face Ridge.

Lot D. Young, a Confederate soldier in the Kentucky Orphan Brigade, watched them come.

> We took positions on the mountain from which we could see extend-
> ing for miles his grand encampment of infantry and artillery, the
> stars and stripes floating from every regimental brigade, division
> and corps headquarters and presenting the greatest panorama I ever
> beheld. Softly and sweetly the music from their bands as they played
> the national airs were wafted up and over the summit of the moun-
> tain. Somehow some way in some inexplicable and unseen man-
> ner, "Hail Columbia" "America" and "The Star Spangled Banner"
> sounded sweeter than I had ever before heard them and filled my
> soul with feelings that I could not describe or forget.[14]

Meanwhile, Sherman sent McPherson through Snake Creek Gap with orders to capture the little town of Resaca and sever Johnston's railroad connection with Atlanta. If successful, this would cut the Confederates from their supply base and perhaps lead to the destruction of their entire army.

McPherson approached Resaca and decided it was too heavily defended for a frontal assault. He pulled back and waited for reinforcements. Whether he made the correct decision has been debated down to the present day, but the result caused major problems for the entire Atlanta campaign. By the time the rest of Sherman's army arrived, the Confederates had fortified the area heavily. Sherman was disappointed at McPherson's caution. As he wrote in his memoirs: "Such an opportunity does not occur twice in a single life."[15]

For the Haworth boys it would be much more than just a missed opportunity.

Nevertheless, Resaca had to be taken.

[May 13, 1864]
On the 13ᵗʰ we marched through Snake Creek gap forme^d^ our Brigade In line of Battle moved up through the timber and tooke a position in the rear of the 14th Army Core pretty heavy fighting gowing on in the front lay thear all night sent some men too the rear next morning to make some coffee General (Henry Moses) Juda was in Command of our Brigade that day He was Drunk

With daylight, Sherman decided to try to outflank Johnston's forces. He moved Schofield's Corps, including the Third Tennessee, to a position where they would be able to assault Resaca directly. Unfortunately, there had been no reconnaissance of what lay ahead. All that anyone knew was that somewhere in front was the rebel army.

at ten o'clock we was ordered to get in line then to fix bayonetes and charge.

Things started to go wrong almost immediately. The terrain was hilly, full of trees and brush. It was impossible to keep the regiments lined up or even to communicate between units. The confusion was compounded by General Cox, whose division was next to Judah's on Schofield's left, being lost with two brigades. Judah mistakenly left one of his three brigades somewhere in the rear.

Waiting for David and his brothers was Philip Daingerfield Stephenson, a private in Company K, Thirteenth Arkansas Volunteer Infantry, CSA. He saw it all.

We were in position very near the point so often attacked . . . so that as the whole scene lay spread before us, we were eye witnesses. We had our hands full with artillery dueling and with the sharpshooters who pestered us exceedingly like bees and wasps and hornets. But at the time of a charge, both sides would stop firing and look on.

Before and to the right of us and immediately in the path of the advancing columns lay a beautiful valley of meadow land, about three

hundred yards in width, dressed in vivid green. It separated the two
ridges on which the opposing forces lay. The woods, dense and black,
reached to the foot of the valley on the enemy's hill. Their trenches
were hidden completely and even their descent to the valley down
their hillside was concealed. When their solid lines of blue broke
suddenly from the woods into view, their banners made gorgeous
flame by the flooding sunlight and sparkles and glitterings flashed
forth from their equipment.

On they come, in three solid lines, in splendid order, bayonets
glancing, banners waving, strains of music pealing, until half across
the valley. Then as by one impulse, they plunge by the double quick
into the charge. At the same instant our ominous silence is broken,
a wild clang of musketry mingles with the thrilling yell of our men,
and the loud and rapid roar of our batteries bursts like a sudden furi-
ous storm upon them! The vast host halts, staggers, the three lines
melt into each other in one confused and reeling mass, then roll back
in dismay, to be swallowed by the woods once more.[16]

The Third Tennessee was ready to fight that day. They charged right
through the regiment in front of them, carrying some of its companies
along with them. General Judah totally lost control of the division as it
swept down the hill toward the waiting Confederates. Far in front of the
other units, Judah's division took the full force of the Confederate fire.

we past through the troops in front of us and charged on the main
rebel fort in front of us we had to cross a little valey and Shuuger
Creek was clost to the fort thear had ^bin^ some small timber on
the banks of the creek the rebels had cut all of that and fell it into
the creek so we could hardly get through. Some of us got ^over^ but
soon had to come back I beleave that I could have walked across
that little field on our dead and Wounded Captin Wm C. Haworth
was at the Head of his Co leading them in the charge Joust at the
edge of the creek he was shot in the head with a minie ball and fell
with part of his boddy in the creek Lieut. Gamble saw his boddey
after he was shot and that night Him ^and^ my Brother I B
Haworth sliped in and got his boddy and carried it out took the

end of cracker box cut his nam ranke & number of regment and dug a grave roled him in his Blanket and buried him

   We was engaged in the charge about 2 hours and our company lost 31 men killed and wounded all of us that got across the creak saw that the rest of our command had stoped in the creek and was sheltering behind the banke and we got back into the creek but our own tropes from the hill was fireing intoo us and the word was past down the line to retreat and I started as fast as I could run backe across the Little field. I was nocked down twice one time a shell came so clost too my head that I fell the next time I had joust steped over a little fence at the edge of the timber a shell burst in the ground By my side and throwed me down again I jumped up and was runing up the hill was nearley up the hill when I turned to get behind a big tree * and a minie ball struck me in the right side just above my hip and knocked me down so I lay where I fell for a while and the rebel bullets were hitting the ground all around me. I crawled up a little to shelter behind a tree. Pretty soon a little doctor came to me with a canteen on. He raised my head and gave me a drink of brandy. He told me he would send the stretcher bearers after me and it wasn't long until two soldiers came running. Rolled me on to the stretcher and carried me back over the top of the ridge. They put me down and I saw General Judah go by so drunk that he was holding to his saddle. He was court-martialed. After that they changed him to some other command.*

*Editor's note: the passage that appears between asterisks was taken from a 1922 typescript of page 105 of David's account, which undoubtedly included edits made by the typist. Page 105 of David's original transcript was lost some years ago.

Seven hundred men of Judah's Division were killed or wounded. He would never again hold a combat command.

*It wasent long untill the Ambulance came and the boys loaded
it up with us wounded they tooke me too ^ the^ field hospital of
the 14th army core it was a large tent they had forks drove in the
ground and plankes lade on them at the end of the tent whear
the Doctors was at work cutting off armes and leegs they laid me
down so that I was faceing that way they would throw the limbs
that was cut off under the table I called one of the boys and told
him too get holt of my blanket and role me over so I could look the
other way Thear was heavy fightting gowing on all the day and
part of the night Joust before night the rebels drove our men back
so far that the Bullets was strikeing around our tent.
about that time reinforcementes came they went by our tent on the
double quick with fixed bayonetes and they drove the rebels out of
Resacca*

Private Stephenson:

Night alone put an end to their dogged pertinacity, and when she
threw her dark pall over the ghastly field, the green little valley
resounded with the cries of the wounded and the dying, while the
members of the infirmary corps flitted like ghosts here and there,
hastily performing their melancholy task.

Just what Sherman's losses were at Resaca, I do not know, but
they were undoubtedly very heavy. Ours were trifling. The prestige
and morale of the affair remained with us, for although we retreated
(compelled by the enemy's ever flanking column) our men were in
the finest spirits and felt that they had gained a victory.[17]

David:

[May 15, 1864]
*Lay thear all the next day on the ground with a few pine boughs
and a Blanket under me got my wound drest for the first time late
on the Second day.*

[May 17, 1864]
On the morning of the 3ʳᵈ day tooke alot of us to Resacca too be
shiped Back to the rear lay thear in a big tent ountill ten oclock
that night when they loaded us intoo a box car whear we lay
ountill tenn oclock the next morning when we started for Chat-
tanooga reaching thear at dark took us all too the field Hospittle
whear we staid for three dayes Eb Simmons is very bad he was
shot through the head Johney Bales come to sea me he was shot
through the right arm flesh wound

Most of the wounded were transported by train with a few boughs and
blankets covering the floor of the car. They did not have springs and the
track was especially rough due to the heavy traffic and lack of mainte-
nance. Trains headed for the front had the right of way, so hospital trains
were often delayed. The wounded suffered greatly.

[May 21, 1864]
On the morning of the 21 ^they^ tooke alot us down and loaded
us into a box car Started out at 2 o'clock. Old General Juda on the
train reached Nashville the next day at 3 oclock tooke me to the
Hospitel no 19 ward 5 thear I got cleaned up and my wound drest
so I felt better then I rote some letters home Elix Morgan and
James Yates come too see me I got a list of the killed and wounded
of our company we lost more men in killed and wounded and
*accompplished the least of aney battle that we was engaged ^in^*
dureing the war I was confined too my room all the time righting
and geteing letters from home and from the boys at the front. I
finly got so I made a few tripes down in town.

[June 15, 1864]
On the 15th my wound was Bleading and so sore that I was con-
fined to my cot on the 22nd I sent up an application for a furlow
too go home then the head doctor come and examed my wound and
he said that I had gangreen in my wound the next day too docters

*come in and told me they was gowing to burn the gangreen out
they wanted ^too^ give me cloreform but I told them I could stand
it they give me all the brandy that I would drink then they puored
the wound full of bromien and it smoked and hurt prettey bad*

Bromine is an element somewhat between chlorine and iodine in its
effects. It would have been a drastic and very painful procedure.

*the Medical director sit by my cot and watched it untill it burnt
the gangreen out then cleaned it out the doctor said it had eat in
too the Strifin. It was varey painful while it lasted I spent the rest
of the month on my cot.*

[July 1, 1864]
*my wond is wors now than it was at the start they eat out so
much rotten flesh that the hole is biger than it was at the start*

[July 7, 1864]
*On the 7 the paymaster come around the surgen of the 119th New
York took charge of our ward my wound is healing up nicely evrey
one out of our ward Except my self and Mcclain of the 33 New
Jersey my furlow came about noon Approved the next day the docters Come in and examed my wound to sea if I was able too make
the trip too Georgetown Illinois whear my parrantes live*

[July 9, 1864]
*they let me start at 5 oclock p.m. of the 9th got to Nashville at 8
oclock staid at the Commercel Hotel all night.*

[July 10, 1864]
*Next morning got Breakfast at the Soldiers Home then I went to
Branch Hospitel No 1 of General Hospitel No 3 thear I found my
Brother John he was shot through the leg below the nee. I staid
with John ountill 3 oclock and at 4 oclock took cars for Lewisville*

Ky got thear the next morning at daylight went too the Soldiers home sent my Furlow to headquarters for transportation and got my wound drest Started for Indianapolis at 2 oclock got thear at 9 oclock that night changed Cars got too Layfayett at 12. Staid thear the rest of the night the next morning started for Danville changed cars at the state line got to Danville at noon put up at

David on leave, recovering from his wounds. He is a different man from that young volunteer who went marching around the flagpole cheering for Uncle Sam. *Author collection.*

the Bradford hous went out and tooke supper with Miss Dunsith
we went too Meeteing at the Methodist church took back next
morning for Georgetown got thear at 7 PM Docter Jenkins drest
my wound then come over home My folkes live 2 miles South of
Georgetown on the Ridge farm road at home all day the next day
Unkle Wm Cannada and Ben and Wesley Kersy come over I am
glad to get home whear I can rest.

[July 17, 1864]
On the 17th went over too town me and Mr. Burns went to church
staid at town for 2 dayes had my photograph taken for Marey and
little Matildey Haworth

[July 20, 1864]
On the 20th I come over home in the male [mail] back Doc drest
my wound that after noon walked over to Unkle Freddy Cana-
days then over too Unkle Wm Canadays whear I staid all night
Marildey and I called on Miss Bell Hastey had a varey pleasant
visit the next morning Asberry Canaday and I come out too the
Ridge farm staid all day having my teeth worked on then rode
over home with Col Baldwin went on to town for the Male
[mail] staid all night next morning me and Mary and Tildy
started over home we met Unkle Isaac Haworth and famly of
Tarrehaut, Indiana we turned back and staid all night come over
home Earley the next morning. We got the glorius newes that our
troopes had captured Atlanta Georga. after noon me and father
walked over to town John Haworth from Indiana come in he
come over home with us and the next day him and I went too
Ridgefarm on the hack we took diner with my old friend Lewis
Thompson and wife Dave little whiped a notorious Copper head
me and John Herrald tooke hand in round up.

Copperheads were a vocal group of Democrats in the North who opposed
the war and agitated for an immediate peace with the South. When the
North was doing badly in the war the Copperhead movement grew. They
opposed the draft, encouraged desertions among Northern troops, called

for Lincoln's defeat at the polls, and blamed the war on abolitionists. But with the fall of Atlanta and the North's improving prospects, the Copperheads began to decline in influence. David's encounter with them must have been quite a melee.

> *I staid all night with Ike Lawrence tooke diner the next day with Thompsons then come over home on the male hack the next day Wes Kersy and famly come we visited all day then father and Mary went too town I went over too Henry Canadys. Asberry Canade and Roos [Rose?] Mendenhall come over. We all went over too Elvin Haworths.*
>
> *Come back too Unkle Freddy Canadays. Staid all night. The next day was Sunday and us boys went over too ^the^ old Vermilion quaker church too Sunday School.*

All over the country Quaker Meetings were still struggling with how to deal with the ongoing war. David does not tell us how the Vermillion Meeting was handling the question, but some meetings, unable to come to terms with their anti-violence beliefs, simply stopped talking about the war.

> *Visit that night at Wm Hesters the next morning me and Mendenhall come over home went on over to town Staid all night up to Aunt Salleys all day the next day helpeing Mary my Brothers widdow, fix up her biziness next day I got Unkle ben Canadays hors and bugey and took mother too Ridge farm we put up at Hereldes and that after noon John and Marion got intoo a fight with a Copper head from down in the hills by the name of Simpson I parted them and came varey near haveing to kill him I had my revolver in my hand and I told him if he ever beat any more of my friends ide get a pass and come back and get him.*
>
> *Then we come back home I went on too town Wm Corvan made a partey for me I took Miss Lida Frasier on the next day went too church it being a day set apart by President Lincon as a*

day of prar and fastening come over home on the 6th Miss Lida
Frazier and Ruth Smith, Reas Mendenhall and Mr. Woodard
come by and we all walked over too Vermillion Quartly meeting
then Lida and I rode up to the ridge farm staid all night with
Lewis Thompson me and Lida talked over quite a lot had a very
pleasant time the next morning I bid them all good by and walked
over home mother and me went over too Mose Runelde had a
good feast of mellons came back I went to town got a letter from
Brother Ike he was wounded on the 26th of July Shot through the
^right arm^ flesh wound My furlow expires to day.
on the 9 I took the hack at half after 11 oclock I stoped in George-
town took diner at Unkle Ben Canadeay Marey and Tildey Zack
Moris and wife were thear me and James K. Richie started for
Danvill at 2 oclocek Got thear before sundown Richie went on to
Indianapolis and I staid all night Tooke my girl too church and
stop in awhile when we come back the next morning at daylight
a speciel train come through with the Twelf Illinois Caveldry they
had bin home on vettern furlow and was gowing to the front.
I got in with them got too Indianapolis at 10 oclock that night
I staid at the Soldiers Home next morning got a train out at 9
oclock got too Jeffersonville next morning at 3 oclock got Breakfast
at the Soldiers home got a train out at 7 traveled all day stood up
most of the way got to Nashville at 5 oclock. got supper at the sol-
diers home then I went out too the hospittle and I found Brother
John and James Collins Staid all night with them and ountill 2
oclock the next day I rote a letter too mother telling her all about
his wound and how he was getting along got started at 2 oclock
got too Murfreesburrow at five oclock went to hospitel No 1 Ward
C. The next day the doctor detaled me as a nurs and from that on
was trying to get sent too my reg

[August 28, 1864]
On the 28th we had general Inspection the docter in charge told me
to get Readdy too go to my co

[August 29, 1864]
The next day had a big scare the report was that generel Wheeler
would attact us all soldiers that can walk was armed and sent too
the fort all wimin and children And government property was
ordered out of town I was in Fort Rosencrance up nearly all night
fighting in the direction of Lavernge

    John Morgan and Whealer are tareing up and burning the
RR on each side of us Capt Smith put me in as Ordley Sargent
and gave me 20 men too gard the gate we was relieved next
morning at 8 oclock and come too camp pretty heavy canonading
in the direction of Nashville 4 thousand Infantry come in that
night on the cars from Chattanooga they marched right through
gowing in the direction of Nashville the next morning at 3 oclock
the rebels fired on our picketes the long Role was beat and evrey
boddy turned out on the 4 the troopes was returning to Chat-
tanooga the RR Co was bringeing up tyes and repareing the RR
they soon had the trains runing. Capt Smith went out forageing
and he brought in 132 rebels that was captured by the 9th Pensel-
vaney Cav all men that belong too No 2 Hospitil ordered back too
the hospitil

[September 7, 1864]
On the 7th we got papers from Nashville saying that General Gil-
lum had surprised and killed John H. Morgan at Greenville East
Tenn the 9th Tenn Caverly has the praise for getting the great
Raider Some of the RR is tore up at Wartrace we get our supplys
and male by wagon trains from Nashville I was detaled too take
12 hundered head of cattle too Telehoma

This was a common detail for Union soldiers. Since there was no practical
way of preserving large amounts of meat for the soldier's rations, herds of
cattle were driven behind the advancing troops. Each day the weakest of
the cattle were slaughtered and pieces handed out to the hungry troops
who then cooked them on their individual campfires. Usually the cattle
had to be driven off the main roads to make room for more essential traf-

fic, so keeping the herds together and moving in the right direction was
no small job.

[September 10, 1864]
*Started out in the morning of the 10th with 33 gardes and 4 dayes
ration theas cattle are Beef Cattle for General Shermans army
we stop in a boddy of timber and grace [graze] them 2 hours at
noon then get a field and put them in at night I put 16 men on
picket I cauled the boys up at 3 oclock and had our cattle moveing
at daylight we stoped at noon in a half mile of Wartrace Correled
the cattle three mile above Wartrace drove into Telahoma the next
day turned over the cattle too the quartermaster then went too the
station had the agent too Flag the freight train we all got on the
box cars and started backe to Murpheysburro ^[unintelligible]^
got thear at noon then I made out my report Company A. and B.
was consolidated I made out a list of the new Company put in the
time Rightting letters.*

[September 15, 1864]
*On the 15th I got orders too get readdy too go too my regiment
I was glad too get the order I boxed up some of my clothes and
expresed them home on the 19th I turned in my gun and at noon
started for the front got on the cars at 5 oclock rode all night on
top of a boxcar got to Chattanooga next morning at 8 oclock went
up too the Convalesent Camp of the first Batalion camped in the
open field No shade no wood nor water vary warm got supper at
the soldiers home and got a train out at 6 oclock rode all night*

[September 21, 1864]
*Got too Big Shantey the morning of the 21st raining had to lay
over waiteing four trains from the frunt too pass then we started
the switch was out of order and our Engin tender and one car
got off of the track when they got them on it was so late the train
backed across the River and thear we staid all night.*

[September 22, 1864]
The next morning at daylight we puled out and got too Atlanta
at 8 oclock Started out to hunt up my Co found them in camp 6
mile below Atlanta not many of my company hear I mes with
A.F. Northern Next day I was sick when our reg went out on
dress perade our Co had only 6 men in line It made me shed tears
too see the onc[e] splendid and large Co now with but 6 men and
myself 2ⁿᵈ Sargent the highyest officer hear

The federal government had advised the adjutant general of Tennessee
that the regiment needed 258 men to bring it up to minimum strength and
asked that he supply them either from volunteers or conscripts.[18]

thear is talk of the 23 Armey Core gowing too Virginia I took
command of our Co on dress perade and order was Read from the
ware department saying that General Spears had bin Dismised
from the servis of the U.S. for not obeying orders of his Superiour
officers no male today the rebels captured the train 2 divisions of
the 4th Army Core gone up too big Shanty the rebel Caverlrey
captured and burnt up 3 trains of cars

Confederate president Jefferson Davis had relieved General Joe Johnston
from command and replaced him with General John Bell Hood. Hood
began an attempt to cut Sherman's supply line to Atlanta by destroying
the railroad.

[September 27, 1864]
Co drill I over hauled the Captins papers. On the 27 we got a big
male. Generl Joe Cooper took command of our division on the 28
the paymaster come in and paid us off I got $114 the RR is tore up
again no male comeing in.

[September 29, 1864]
*On the 29th I.I. Troutman and Henry Overbay of our Co came
up Had Batalion drill Lieutenent Armstrong of Co A was ordered
too take command of our Company the rebels have tore ^up^ a lot
of the RR at Dalton so we dont have any trains*

Forced out of Atlanta, John Bell Hood devised a daring strategy. He doubled back northwest, planning to cut Sherman's railroad supply lines and force him to follow. Hood hoped to fight and defeat Sherman somewhere in the mountains. If Sherman failed to follow, Hood would attack and recapture Nashville and then, perhaps, head east to join up with Lee's army. It was a desperate gamble, but on September 29, preceded by Forrest's cavalry tearing up railroad and telegraph lines, Hood moved.

[October 1864]
*Raining about all day I Sarget and one man for picket Drawed 5
dayes rations the regiment started out at 6 oclock forageing Jacob A.
Troutman reported for duty also James H. Lewis all of the Sick or
disabled ordered too Atlanta the order come too strike tentes and
Be readey too march at one oclock order countermanded we staid
on our old camp ground All night hauling all of our extry bagage
too Atlanta.*

[October 4, 1864]
*The next morning we marched out Early went out on the road
leadeing too the Chattahocha Railroad Bridge Marched hard
all day in the rain through a desolate lookeing country all cut up
with rifle pites and on every hill A part crost the river and went
into camp that night at 10 oclock. Oct 5 we marched out Earley
and marched hard all day past through Marietta and ruff Station
marched ountill 10 clock at nigh drawed some Beef we have bin
without rations for 2 days Except crackers We camped in the open
field raining all night Slept on the ground roled up in our blankets
water under us. Not a rale nor chunk too make a fire.*

As soon as Sherman realized that Hood's entire army was on the move, he followed him north, fighting a series of inconclusive engagements and avoiding numerous ambushes. But he was frustrated at the prospect of continuing the pursuit of Hood.

[October 6, 1864]
Started on at 8 oclock rained until 12 oclock we got in 4 mile of Acworth turned back and camped in the rebel Brestworks we have changed positions one man for picket on the 7th the sun shined and was drying our Blanketes and clothing prettey heavey fighting off too our left we ar after old Hood he seames too want too go too Nashvill we drawed 2 dayes rations the 3rd Division out Recunortering our Core the 23 Armey Core commanded by General Scofield is following Hood orders to be ready too march in the morning

[October 8, 1864]
Never got started ountill 3 oclock we struck the RR at Acworth the RR all tore up and cross ties are burnt up we camped that night at Altoona [Allatoona] Station we have a Big lot of supplies stored hear this was one of Shermans supply stations October the 8th we went into camp that night at 9 oclock near Altoona station. I mess with M.F. Price the next day we was in camp all day near the battle ground of the 5th inst went over in town and went all over the battle ground the part on the west side was whear the hardest fightting was a rebel Division charged 5 times they were Hungry and wanted the provisions that was stored thear in thoes big ware Houses.

The battle on October 5 took place at a fortified supply base near Alla-toona. The Confederates made a desperate effort to capture the fort but were unsuccessful. The cost in dead and wounded was dreadful on both sides: 705 for the Union forces and 800 for the Confederates. But the three million rations were saved.

*The company that defended that fort berried 13 of thear number
in one grave this was 5 dayes after the Battle and thear dead was
laying whear they fell. And in frunt of that fort they was piled
up the wounded had bin gathered up. evrey hous and barn was
full they had no docters until we come our docters went too worke
takeing the worst cases first I counted 13 dead laying beside the
road they looked awful Big we marched out fast through Cas Station. Crost Eatovah camped at Casville*

[October 10, 1864]
*Next morning marched out on quick time past through Cassville
fighting at rome past through Kingston tooke the road leading
too Rome Stoped and went intoo camp within 12 mile of Rome
drawed one days rations*

[October 11, 1864]
*Moved out Early next morning marched hard camp within one
mile of Rome fighting gowing on Across the River drawed 3 days
rations Marched out at 6 oclock Marched through Rome crost the
Oostenolla [Oostenaula] river went out on the Ceder Bluff road
we found Wilder's brigade of rebel caverly formed in line of battle
across our road we put out a heavy skirmish line and engaged
them while we was geting in line then the order was fix Bayonets
and charge we went at them with a yell and we captured 2 peases
of artillery And 30 prisners I Saw 9 of thear men Dead whear we
got the Artilry come back and camped on our old camp ground*

[October 14, 1864]
*on the 14th marched out at 7 o'clock tooke the road leading too
Calhoon marched varey slow the 4th and 14th Army Coors are in
frunt of us we went intoo camp at 10 oclock at night thear is not a
hous barn or fence left standing in this part*

[October 15, 1864]
Next morning moved out at 6 I sent M F Price and W H
Statham too the Ambulance sicke past through Calhoon stoped
for diner one mile above then crost the oostenolla river Marched
through Resacca tooke the Snake Creek Gap Road went intoo
camp one mile and a half near the battle field of the 14th of last
May whear the Remains of my brother W^m C Haworth is berried
Addam Northern our flag barrier is sicke I carey the flag stopped
in Snake Creek gap to get diner camped at Chattahooch Valey on
the side of rockey face Mounten drawed rations at 10 oclock at
night Burnt a hous too make a light

[October 17, 1864]
The next morning our reg and 90th Ohio was detaled as gard
for a forageing train went down the valley about 3 miles got some
corn Me and Mark Price got two canteens of Sargum and some
sweat potatoes and chesnuts come back camped on our old camp
ground All of our army resting the trains comeing in

[October 18, 1864]
On the 18 we marched out at 5 oclock down the Valey road leading
too Summervill marched hard all day past the train of the 17th
Armey Core crost through Wilson's gap the rebels Blasted off and
Blockaded the road but we cleared it out camped at 8 at Night 2
rebel soldiers came in and surrendered we peroled them we past
through a beutiful valey

[October 19, 1864]
Early the next the 2^ed and third Division of Cavelry past our
camp then at 11 oclock we marched out crost the Chattahootia
river past too the left of Summerville past the 15th Army core and
went intoo camp drawed rations marched out the next morning at
daylight. Crost the Chattahootia river again past through Gales-
ville cherokee County Alabamie. Stoped for dinner on piney Creek
then about 2 oclock moved out about 30 ydes and camped fur

*the night we have past through a beutiful valey and evrey thing
lookes fine*

[October 20, 1864]
*In camp all day the next day washing and cleaning up. Mark
Price went over Skin Bone Ridge foraging got potatoes chickens
and turnips the 3rd Brigade went out foraging they found 3 men
Belonging too the 65 Indiana hung over in the valey*

[October 24, 1864]
*In camp ountill today the 24 when we moved up too Ceder bluff
Our Brigade went up the river 4 miles and camped I tooke 10
men and went on picket*

[October 25, 1864]
*Broke camp next morning at daylight four Ceder bluff Stoped in
the edge of town Stacked arms the 6th come up with Generel Scofield we marched through town at 3 oclock crosed the Coosey river
on the pontoon Bridge throwed up some rifle pites with Rails and
dirt order to be ready too march next morning.*

[October 26, 1864]
*the 2cd Brigade of the third Division crost the river early went out
south and was soon engaged with the rebel Cavelrey they drove
them 5 miles then come Back too camp*

[October 27, 1864]
*The male come in on the 27th our regment and the 25th Michigan
went out garding the forageing train met the rebels out about 3
miles right in the road we had it pretty livley fur awhile we drove
them ^off^ and got our forage*

[October 28, 1864]
*The next morning we struck tentes the 3rd Division past by All of
the 23 Armey Core wagon trains and the 15th and 17 army core
trains crost over. we lay in camp all day*

[October 29, 1864]

Moved out the next morning at daylight our Division gard-
ing the wagon trains our Brigade in the rear the Roads are cut
up wagons mire down and we help role them out we strucke the
Road leading too Room and camped four Diner we camped at
Martans store at 9 oclock at night we are in 4 miles of the Georga
State Line

[October 30, 1864]

Moved out the next morning early past through Cave Spring a
butiful little vilage Camped on Ceder Creek fur diner went into
camp within 2 miles of Rome we got male moved out at daylight
Crost the river on the pontoon Bridge marched through rome crost
the Hitower river marched out on the road leading too Calhoon
marched hard all day John M. Leeper and Wm C. Webster of our
Co come too us went intoo camp within 5 miles of Calhoon hear
we drawed cloathing Marched at daylight Crost Oootheload
Creek marched through Calhoon and resacca went into camp and
drawed 5 days rations of evrey thing Except bread Raining and
cold no wood and no fire rained all day and night

[November 2, 1864]

The 3rd Brigade gone to guard the wagon train tonight. On the
night of the 2^cd our Brigade was loaded intoo box cars and on top

[November 3, 1864]

Got to Dalton the next morning raining and cold our reg all
except Companys A F D ride on top of the cars no bread tooday
past through tunel hill and ringgold Joust stoped long enuf at
chattanooga to draw Crackers rode all night on top of the cars
raining and pretty cold

[November 6, 1864]

Got to Steveeson next morning got off and made some coffee rode
on top of the cars too Telehoma then we changed got inside past
through Murfreesburrow at dark got too Nashville at 10

oclock went right on too Johnstonville rode all night on top of the cars. Varey cold..

[November 7, 1864]
Meeteing men off of the gun ^boat^ the rebels sunke lotes of people fleeing from the rebel cavarldry our brigade got off of the cars at the edge of town which is most all burnt up our Co marched right down mane streat too the banke of the Tennessee rive thear was some big ware houses that hadent bin burnt we scattered out and tooke positions in the ware houses and began picking off the men that was on the other banke we soon Drove the artilrey off the rest of our men went up on the hill and planted the canon Soon had the rebels all back away from the river then our troopes went too fortefiing and bilding a fort on the hill worked all day and night the 99 Ohio come in with generel Scofield.

[November 8, 1864]
The next day Nate Milles was left at Chattanooga sick. part of the 2cd Brigade come in with Generl Scofield

[November 9, 1864]
On the 9th we all went down in town. Drawed clothing and rations this Being Election day we all voted for president and vis president I voted fur Abraham Lincoln for president and Andrew Johnson fur vis president not a vote in our reg cast for McClelon 4 men too work on the fort Nate Miles come too the Co. Col Moore in command of the post the 14th Kentucky Infanry strucke tentes and are gowing home too [be] mustered out of the servis General Joe Cooper come up rote some letters home drawed rations

[November 10, 1864]
Next day 4 men for fatigue. Lieut Buckalew and Ephram Tabler come up verry windy and cold. Half of our men for too work on the fort and picket duty evrey day

After chasing Hood's army through northern Georgia and part of Alabama, with little result, Sherman decided to leave the task of dealing with Hood to General Schofield and the defense of Nashville to General Thomas. He took most of his forces back to Atlanta and prepared to leave on his historic "march to the sea." Schofield moved his headquarters south of Nashville to Pulaski, while Hood moved west toward the Georgia state line. The Third Tennessee remained with Schofield's command.

[November 23, 1864]
On the 23rd me and Mark Price and Dave Cokenour split timber and bilt us a little hous with chimly that nigt got ordered too be readdy too march early next morning we was up part of the nigt Drawing rations and me and my brother Ike was over hauling the Captins papers we tooke the importend papers and we carried them with us.

[November 24, 1864]
Ready to march next morning at daylight then order come too burn evrey thing that cant take with us so our new little Winter quarters went up in the flames and we moved out gowing up the R R too Weaverley thear we took the road leading too Centerville I gave out come into camp at 10 oclock.

[November 25, 1864]
Orders was too be ready too march at Daylight but never started ountill 11 oclock AM Waded Duck river and went intoo camp Before sundown drawed rations raining Most of the night and all of the next day

Schofield's move south to Pulaski allowed Hood to get between him and Nashville, but by the narrowest of margins the Union forces were able to get past the Confederate troops and dig in at Franklin on the road north.

[November 26, 1864]

moved out early all men that havent guns too stay with the wagons too help role them out of Mud holes Marched ountill after dark me and Dunlap gave out we slept in an old barn in site of our camp

[November 27, 1864]

Marched out at 10 oclock Crost Piney Creek our regiment in the rear of all of the wagons our Co and Co B and G was rear gard Ik stoped too fill his canteen at a creek And got behind a Bushwacker dashed up and like to captured him Camped within 1/2 mile of harpeth river had a Skirmish with some rebel caverlly

[November 28, 1864]

next morning marched early our regiment in the frunt Marched slow gathering up Horses and Mules After noon we marched hard went intoo camp at a ford on the river orders that we will gard this ford fur 3 or 4 dayes put up our tents no rations 2 men fur picket on sargt and 25 picked men with a citizen gid. All mounted started with a dispatch fur Generel Scofield at Columbia Tenn drawed rations all of our Brigade Scattered up and down the river gardeing the Fordes

[November 29, 1864]

On the after noon of the 29th we could hear the artilrey at Franklin. The battle is on.

Hood caught up with Schofield's army at Franklin and, despite the fact that the Union troops had managed to quickly construct a strong defensive position, he decided to make a desperate frontal charge. The result was a disaster: 4,500 Confederate casualties, including fourteen general officers. Schofield quietly left Franklin, moved inside Nashville's already strong defensive lines, and waited.

[November 30, 1864]
On the next day Lieut. Buckalew with 20 men went down the
river with a wagon too get some flower our pickets was fired on
we drove them off.

Hood continued on to Nashville, desperately hoping for some victory. He
told his men to make "a last manful effort to lift up the sinking fortunes
of the Confederacy."

[December 1864]
We started for Nashville at 12 oclock. Never stoped ountill 9 oclock
at night No water all day Our Co is the advance gard. We caught
up with the 130th Indiania and the 99 ohio. raining most all
night. Marched out at Sunup. Order are fur man to keep every
man too his place; and to Load our guns. Joust at darke we strucke
the granny white pike. Hoodes army had come in on this pike and
was now betwean us and Nashvill. We captured thear picketes,
then we turned back and started for Clarkesville on the Cum-
berlan river. We had a Citizen gide. We traveled down Harpeth
river marched hard all night.

[December 2, 1864]
passed dog creek at daylight our reg joust had one wagon and
when we turned back the driver broke the tung and left the
wagon on the pike Captain Wm C. Haworth bookcase and most all
of his papers and my knapsac was in that wagon

[December 3, 1864]
We waded Harpeth River and stoped for breakfast nothing too eat
but a little flower marched hard all day went into camp at Sharlet
no rations have too live off of the countrey and not much too get I
sliped down in town and got some Bread

[December 4, 1864]

marched out next morning at 8 oclock varey sore and tirred marched vary hard went intoo camp at darke Co. K G an B rear gard we ar within 13 miles of Clarkesville

[December 5, 1864]

Next morning marched at daylight our regment in the rear. Our Co on picket while our Brigade is crosing the river Joust one little steam boat to get us across. We come over joust at night marched through Clarkesville And went into camp Drawed rations and good corn whiskey the Nashville paper had Published that ^Hood^ had captured our Brigade we was 4 dayes and nightes after we left the graney white Turnpike ountill we crostthe Cumberlan River at Clarkesville

[December 6, 1864]

the next Day we shot the loads out of our guns and cleaned them up and rested. Most of the boys gone too town the Second Tenn Mt Infantry went by gowing too Nashville we now have plenty to eat and Drink

[December 7, 1864]

on the morning of the 7th we started fur Nashville at 5 oclock Drizeling rain all day went intoo camp after marching 25 miles cold and windey

The opposing armies were watching each other at Nashville. General George Thomas, who commanded the city's defenses, was under pressure from Grant to attack and finish Hood off, but he refused to do so until his forces were fully ready. He was particularly anxious to get remounts for his cavalry.

[December 8, 1864]

Marched at five o'clock on the 8th varey windey and cold all day

Camped in Edgefield But little wood most of the men havend any Blanketes I have one blanket

[December 9, 1864]
moved out on the 9 at 8 oclock Crost the river intoo Nashville on the R R Bridge Sleateing and Freezeing Marched through town Camped too the right of fort Negley no wood I staid in town

In one of those ironic twists so common in war, Private William Daingerfield Stephenson, the Confederate soldier who faced the Haworth brothers at Resaca, was once again opposite them under the ominous guns of Fort Negley. Stephenson wrote:

Our battery had moved forward . . . and I found it on the Nolansville Pike immediately in front of the famous Fort Negely which easily commanded our insignificant works . . . Every indication pointed to preparations for an assault by our foe. The bustle, the activity of their skirmishers, the increased shelling from their forts, these and other signs showed that they meant mischief very soon.[19]

No doubt "mischief" was in the making, but at that point David Haworth was just trying to stay warm and dry.

[December 10, 1864]
Come too camp next morning no wood

[December 11, 1864]
Me and A.F. Northern and Brother ^Ike^ went back ^too^ town next day. Working on some riful pites all day the rebel fortifyfica-tions [sic]are in site

[December 12, 1864]
we had some skirmishing on the 12 our caverley that has bin camped back of Edgefield Began moving out too the frunt they

are concentrateing on our right wing we drawed 4 days rations
and got orders too be readdy too march at 5 oclock tomorrow we
are gowing to try too move Hoodes army

[December 13, 1864]
Didnt move out today the ground was covered with ice and so
fogey varey cold and fogey one man for picket 2 men too drive
some beef cattle one too worke with the pioneers [prisoners?]
John Maples came too the company we got the word that Generel
Steadmans Division of Coulered troopes was gowing too charge
on the rebel workes Joust About noon the big gunes in fort Negley
commenced sheling the rebel workes in frunt of Steadmans troopes
then all of our Artilrey too our left joined in we all got out whear
we could see that lasted fur about one hour then they all quit and
then we could sea Steadmans Division in 2 lines of Battle with
fixed Bayonetes charge across the little valey they got up clost too
the rebel fort But finley had too come backe late that Day they
went under a flag of truce and brought off their dead and wonded.

Private Stephenson watched the same charge, but with a particularly
Southern point of view.

(The battle) began with a general cannonade along the whole front.
Under cover of the smoke several bodies of troops were moved forward on both wings . . . This was the first time that we of the Army
of Tennessee had ever met our former slaves in battle. It excited in
our men the intensest indignation, but that indignation expressed
itself in a way peculiarly ominous and yet quite natural for the "masters." As soon as it was found out that the men advancing upon them
were Negroes, a deliberate policy was adopted. It was to let them
come almost to the works before a shot was to be fired, and then the
whole line was to rise up and empty their guns into them. On they
came, closer and closer . . . then up rose the line of grey and crash
went that deadly volley of lead full into the poor fellow's faces. The
carnage was awful.[20]

David or someone in his regiment at some point managed to retrieve the
wagon full of William C. Haworth's papers. David:

[December 14, 1864]
The next day our regiment went back acros the Cumberland river
and got some wood then I boxed up all of Captin Wm C. Haworths
papers too send home put them in charge of lieutenant Saphel too
Express. orderes that we be ready too march tomorrow morning at
5 oclocke

[December 15, 1864]
We was up at 4 got a little Breakfast and moved out at 5 oclocke
General Thomases Army is geteing in position too move on
Hoodes armey that is prettey strongley forteyfied all on the South
of Nashville we marched down too our right inside of our riful
piets we crost the Graney White pike and went too the next pike
whear our Caverley was gowing out thear we formed line and
lay down too the Southeast of us the rebels had 4 peases of Artilry
at a big Brick hous and they was shelling the caverly as they went
out we was ordered too goo over the workes and form in a draw
about half way too the bricke hous we went in on the run stoped
in the little valey and formed in line of battle fixed Bayonets and
charged on the fort we captured all 4 peases and about half of the
regiment that was supporting them this was joust our Brigade in
this charge then Generel Couch joined us with the Ballance of our
Division then we put out a double skirmish line then we faced
back east and Commenced crumplin up the rebel lines we came
to the Graney White pike thear was a fort on the east of the pike
and heavy riful pites off on our right with a lot of rebel Infantry
behing [behind] a stone fence the 24th Kentucky with some caverly
was sent too get them and they soon come gardeing them too the
rear then we made a charge fur the batterry on the hill and we
finley captured the gunes and most of the support. It was a hard
fight; them guners never quit ountill we went over the top. It was
soon darke. I was Sent with a detal too gather up the wonded and
carry them down too the turnpike whear the ambulances could get

them. I found Brother Ike and sent him ^too^ a hospitel in Nash-
vill. he was shot in the right arm; flesh wond. we got the boys that
was wounded gatherd up and sent in by midnight, then we joined
our Co. our 23 Army Core was all workeing diging riful pites on
the side of a hill faceing the rebel workes joust acros on the other
side. we worked hard all night.

[December 16, 1864]
When daylight come the Sharp Shooters began had too keep
down or get hurt. The word was past down the line from Generel
Thomas that our Caverelry had gone around Hoodes left wing
and would attack on his rear. the signel of that attack was too be
the fireing of a hole batterrey on gulfes hill at one time; then every
piece of artilry was to shell the rebel workes while the infantry
was too charge. Thear we lay all day watching and listening. Joust
before sun down the big guns belched forth and every canon that
we had responded. It seamed too pike up the earth and over the top
we went. The rebels never saw us infantry. The shells was keepe-
ing them down. When we was up prettey clost too thear workes
our canon stoped then they opened up some but we went over the
top so qwick they didn't doe much. they seamed glad to surrender.

Private Stephenson:

All things were at once abandoned. The wildest confusion and
terror took hold of the men. Each individual looked to himself . . .
the plunging steeds of the officers, the incoherent cries of our panic
stricken infantry as they rushed among us, the piteous entreaties of
our wounded not to leave them, the vast heap and ruined debris of
the army machinery all around us, the fearful storm above and about
us. Ah, that was a picture![21]

David:

*That night it was raining and cold all night and the dead and
wonded lay on the field all night. we tore out the railes and logs
of the riful pites and made Fires and I was geteing something too
Eat. I saw a rebel Soldier boy crawling up too my fire. he had bin
shot through the leg his leg was broke when I got too him he looked
up and saw on the frunt of my cap the letters 3ʳᵈ Tenn Vol Inft.
He throwed up his hand and ses fur godes sake don't kill me. I told
him thear was no occasion too kill him fur the ware would be over
before he would be able too fight aney more. he said thear officers
told them that us Tennesee soldiers killed all the prisners that we
captured. I got him up clost too the fire divided coffee and grub
with him. got a gum blanket; spread it over him too keep the rain
off. I roled up in my blanket and sleap all night. was wore out
never sleap any last night.*

[December 17, 1864]
*We was called up at daylight had nothing too eat went out on the
battle field got some [food] out of haversacke of thoes that couldent
use it. I again divided grub and before I left him I got a canteen
went too a branch filed it and sit by him.
then we moved out after the retreating rebels. we captured five
thousand prisners and twenty seven peases of artilerry yesterday.
Entirely routing Hoodes armey. we moved out within half a mile
of the franklin Turnpike and went intoo camp. Lotes of prisners
comeing back. raining all day and awful muddey. the pike is wore
out. we have too help role the wagons and artilry out of mud holes
on the pike.*

[December 18,1864]
*On the 18ᵗʰ marched early. Stoped and drawed rations when we
come up too the wagon train. marched all day in the mud sometimes over our shoe top. meeteing prisners all day. One stand of
culors and 3 canon camped in site of Franklin in an open field.
raining all night. no wood.*

[December 19, 1864]

Marched at daylight following up the remnent of Hoodes army. They are in full retreat. rained all day. all men that havent any guns too stay with the wagon train too help role them up the steep hills and out of mud holes. marched ountill after dark. Me and Joe Dunlap give out and was left behind. We come up in site of our camp. Stoped at a farm hous and got something too eat then we got up in the loft of a log barn that stood clost too the road. found some straw and was soon asleap Sometime in the night we was awaken by the fireing of gunes. Some Rebel caverley had attacted Captin Bingham who was in command of our pickets not varey far above whear we was. We got ready and as they went backe we fired intoo them through the crack. One of them hollored like he was hurt but never got aney of them off; then we laid down and went to sleep again.

[December 20, 1864]

we got out earley and went intoo camp. remained in camp ountill 12 oclock then we moved out crost Harpeth river. Steddey rain all day. marched through Franklin; the churches and evury publice hous filed with woonded. we went intoo camp one mile out in the timber. we had plentey of railes and wood too burn. Drying our blanketes and clothing. Henry H. Troutman broke his arm over again.

[December 21, 1864]

readey too march at daylight but never moved ountill 10 oclock. Went out on the Columbia Pike. raining all day; turned to sleat- ing. Camped within one mile of Spring Hill. Snowed most all night. one man fur picket.

[December 22, 1864]

the next morning we drawed rations And made out a try mon- thelly report. Varey cold. Snowing all morning. marched out at one oclock on the double qwick. Past the 16 and 17 Armey cors and the third Division of our caverllry and all of the wagon trains

*marched 6 miles and camped at Duck river whear we staid fur
2 dayes waiting for the pontoon Bridge to be put across the river.
Drawed rations. ordered to strike tentes. Generel Scofield with
the 3rd Division moved too Calumbia then ordered too put up our
tentes. Cold and clear*

[December 25, 1864]
*The 16th Armey Core received orders yesterday too gow back too
Nashville. we spent Chrismas day in camp all day. Our male
come in I got 3 letters. a varey quiet and lonley day. we drawed
Rotations late in the day.*

On December 24, John Bell Hood and the remnants of his army crossed
the Tennessee River headed south. Only twenty thousand of his men
remained. The rest had been killed, wounded, or captured at Franklin and
Nashville. The only significant military force left to the Confederacy was
Lee's at Richmond.

[December 26, 1864]
*Called out early next morning. Moved out at 9 oclock. Went intoo
camp on the bluff oposit Calumbia in the old Rebel camp.*

[December 27, 1864]
*Next day was raining and cold. we struck tentes marched down
and went intoo camp joust above the R R Bridge on the Bluff.
ordered too have role call.*

*we remained in this camp all the Ballance of December. on the
29th drawed 3 days rations. made out monthley report. the first
division come in Hoodes Armey crost the Tenn river at Musel
Sholes. four hundred Rebel prisners went on too the rear. one man
to gard the prisners*

CHAPTER FOUR
~ 1865 ~

[January 1, 1865]
January found us in camp on duck river. Snow on the ground. I took Jacop A. Troutman too the hospitel. got our male Drawed rations. I rote too Z Moris. Marched out at 9 oclock. The 99th ohio and the 50th ohio infantry of our brigade was Consolidated. we crost Duck river. Marched through Calumbia. marched out on the road leading to Cliften on the Tennisee river. I give out. Camped that night on West fork creeke. One man fur picket.

[January 2, 1865]
Moved out next morning at half after 7 oclock. about noon we left the turnpike. past through Mount pleasont. varey muddey roades. part of Hoodes army went this way. we camped before sundown in a rebel camp. I went too the Ambulance and got Troutman.

[January 3, 1865]
Marched out earley. our Brigade in the frunt. Past through Henryville. went into camp at noon drawed rations one man too work the road. Col. Cross gone in command of the detale.

[January 5, 1865]
On the 5th we marched out at daylight. Marched hard all day. our Brigade in the rear. Joust at night we come in by side of the third Division of our Core and we had a race too camp. we camped one mile above Wains Burrow. George B. Smith come up. Generel McClain and Generl Scofield past by ring guard put around our brigade. one man too go forageing. the Third Division moved on. Col. Cross came in with the prisniers. the first division camped joust below. Snowing and sleating.

[January 7, 1865]
Laying in camp all day of the 7th.

[January 8, 1865]
Marched out at 6 ½ next morning. past through Wains burrow.
no rations. went intoo camp within three mile of Clifton. Had
rool call before brakeing ranks. no rations hear.

[January 9, 1865]
Jan the 9th cold drizelly rain all day. the first division past by.
laying most all day in my tent. rote a letter too Mother. Made out
a try monthley report. I have a bade headach today. orders to be
readey too march in the morning.

[January 10, 1865]
The bugel sounded before Daylight. Tore down our tentes in a
thunder and rain storm. Marched too Cliften or whear it use too
bee. Camped on the right near the Tennessee river. rained and
snowed all day. drawed 2 days rations of Beef. No Bread. Detailed
one man to load wagons on the barges. 3 steamboates come up after
dark.

[January 11, 1865]
Next day cold and windy. no rations ountill noon; then we
drawed 3 days rations. laying in camp all day. We remained in
camp at Clifton ountill about the 25th. we had orders too get ready
to goo too meat Generl Sherman in North Carolina. Had all of
our supplys, amunition, Wagons, Artilrey and Horses loadid ontoo
barges and steamboates and would have started the next morn-
ing and that night we received order too gow too Nashville too be
mustered out. we loaded onto a steamboat next day and started
down the Tennessee river at Cairo. When we got intoo the Ohio
river the amber ice was pretty dangerus. We joust had 12 miles up
the Ohio too the mouth of the Cumberland river.

[February 1, 1865]
We ounloaded in Nashville about the first of Febuary. we marched through town and went intoo camp near Fort Negley. In a few days we moved too the Tennisse barracks and remained thear while they was geteing readey too muster us out of the servis. We was mustered out on the 24 of Feb 1865. Disharged and paid Feb 28th 1865.

[March 1, 1865]
I left Nashville Tenn on March the 1st four Georgetown Illinois whear my Father and Mother with part of our family was live-ing. the rebels had drove my father out of the state Becaus he had 4 of us boyes in the Union army. also my brothers wife and little girl was at Georgetown. I got home on March 5ᵗʰ. Staid thear outill May 22 when I started with Father and famly, Marey and Matildey gowing Back too our old home in Jefferson County East Tennissee.

[May 1865]
When we got too Nashville I went too the State Hous and called on oold Parson Brownlow. he was Military Governor of Tenn. He new me. I staid all night with him when he lived in Cin-cinnatta ohio. He gave all of us ticketes and free transportation for our Bagage too our homes and gave me ^a^ speciel permit to carry armes fur home or individiul protection. They arrived at home on May 28 and I got home on June the 4th. I stoped over at Knoxville a few days. My father had four hundred acres of land but when we come back we found the farm in bad condition. My Brother Wᵐ C Haworth Captin of Co K 3ʳᵈ ten was killed at the battle of Resacca Georga. 3 of us wounded twice apeas.

David does not mention the attitude of their neighbors, but they had forced the family to flee to Illinois, and the fact that Parson Brownlow felt it necessary to give David a pistol for "home and personal protection" spoke volumes.

David and his brothers did what they had to do. They participated in preserving the Union and eliminating slavery from that Union. But it came at a terrible price. The first-born son was killed, the other three seriously wounded multiple times, the farm homestead was lost, and the remainder of the Haworth family reduced to refugees.

The Quakers had struggled with their twin impossible goals: eliminating slavery and avoiding violence. The Haworth boys were literally running for their lives when they escaped into Kentucky and joined the Union army. For others in the North it was a personal choice. Not for the Haworths. So, in the end, what was to be said?

Perhaps it was summed up best in the eulogy for a Quaker soldier who had been killed in action:

> To make war in his country forever impossible by eradicating human slavery, its permanent cause, he took up arms. There seemed to be no other way of doing it. He would thankfully have used other means had other means been permitted. . . . You need not be afraid of shocking your principles by receiving him here from battle. . . . Do we hate war less in these days than formerly? Nay, Friends, we hate it, if possible, a thousand times more, when we see them, father and son, doing such deeds as this. [22]

Some of the Haworth family remained to East Tennessee, but David and his brothers moved on to Lawrence County in Southwestern Missouri. There they lived out their lives, raising large families and dying peacefully in their old age.

NOTES

1. Ulysses S. Grant, *Personal Memoirs of U. S. Grant* (New York: Charles L. Webster & Co., 1886), 145.

2. *Official Records,* Series I, Vol. 10 (later abbreviated *OR*) pp 563-564

3. *Official Records,* Series I, Vol. 10, Pt. II: 640-641.

4. *Official Records* Series I, Vol. 10, Pt. II: 682.

5. *Official Records,* Series I, Vol. 10, pt. II: 429.

6. *Official Records,* Series II, Vol. 4: 122-123.

7. *Official Records,* Series II, Vol. 1: 890.

8. *Mobile Register and Advertiser,* September 1, 1861.

9. *Mobile Register And Advertiser,* September 1, 1861.

10. *Nashville Union,* July 22, 1864.

11. *Official Records,* Series I, Vol. 32, pt. III: 226.

12. Lloyd Lewis, *Sherman: Fighting Prophet* (New York: Harcourt, Brace and Company, 1932), 355.

13. Lot D. Young, *Reminiscences of a Soldier of the Orphan Brigade* (Louisville: Courier Journal Job Printing, ca. 1918), 34.

14. Young, *Reminiscences,* 35.

15. Lewis, *Fighting Prophet,* 357.

16. Philip Daingerfield Stephenson, *The Civil War Memoir of Philip Daingerfield Stephenson D. D.* (Conway, AR: UCA Press, 1995), 175-176.

17. Stephenson, *The Civil War Memoir,* 176.

18. *Official Records,* Vol. 38, Part III: 638-684.

19. Stephenson, *The Civil War Memoir,* 319.

20. Stephenson, *The Civil War Memoir,* 322.

21. Stephenson, *The Civil War Memoir,* 331.

22. Reverend O.B. Frothingham, "Words Spoken at the Funeral," excerpted from A. J. H. Duganne, *The Quaker Soldiers, A True Story of the War for our Union* (New York: J.P. Robens, 1869), 107. Located at ramwebs.wcupa.edu/jones/his480/reports/civilwar.htm.

BIBLIOGRAPHY

Books

Bowman, John S. *The Civil War Day By Day*. Greenwich, CT: Brompton Boks.

Cannan, John. *The Atlanta Campaign*. Conshohocken, PA: Combined Books, Inc., 1991.

Cox, Jacob D. *Sherman's Battle For Atlanta*. New York: Da Capo Press, 1994.

Eicher, David J. *The Longest Night: A Military History Of The Civil War*. New York: Simon & Schuster, 2002.

Grant, U. S. *Personal Memoirs of U. S. Grant*. New York: Charles L. Webster & Co., 1886.

Groom, Winston. *Shrouds Of Glory*. New York: The Atlantic Monthly Press, 1995.

Lewis, Lloyd. *Sherman, Fighting Prophet*. New York: Harcourt, Brace and Company, 1932.

Macdonald, John. *Great Battles of the Civil War*. New York: Macmillan Publishing Co., 1988.

Secrist, Philip L. *The Battle Of Resaca*. Macon, GA: Mercer University Press, 1998.

Sherman, William T. *Memoirs of General W. T. Sherman*. New York: D. Appleton & Co., 1875.

Stephenson, Philip Daingerfield. *The Civil War Memoir of Philip Daingerfield Stephenson, D. D.* Conway, AR: UCA Press, 1995.

War Of The Rebellion: A Compilation Of The Official Records Of The Union And Confederate Armies. Washington, DC, 1880–1901.

Tennesseans In The Civil War. Nashville: Part I Centennial Commission, 1964.

Ward, Jeoffrey C. *The Civil War*. New York: Alfred A. Knopf, 1990.

Young, Lot D. *Reminiscences Of A Soldier Of The Orphan Brigade*. Louisville: Courier Journal Job Printing, ca. 1918.

Newspapers

Mobile Register and Advertiser

Nashville Union

ABOUT THE EDITOR

A native of Neosho, Missouri, Gene Allen graduated from Oklahoma State University. While still in school, he began a career in broadcasting, writing copy for several small-town radio stations. With the advent of television he moved to WKY-TV, Oklahoma City, writing and producing a number of award-winning documentaries. He lives in Oklahoma City with his wife Cheryl.

Gene Allen. *Family collection*

INDEX

Seventy-Third Illinois Infantry regiment, 27

Shelby, Col., 45

Sherman, William Tecumseh, 84–85, 91, 103; Atlanta Campaign of (1864), 68–74; "March to the Sea" of, 91; on Parson Brownlow, 34; given Union command of Western theater, 66, 67

Simmons, Eb, 75; stabbing of, 46

Sixteenth Ohio Infantry regiment, 41

Sixth Tennessee Infantry regiment, 38, 41, 44, 45, 47, 48

Sixty-Fifth Indiana Infantry regiment, 88

Sixty-Ninth Ohio Infantry regiment, 43

slavery: Quakers on, 3, 11, 105; in Tennessee, 1

Slover, Capt., 51

smallpox, 55

Smith, Capt., 81

Smith, George B., 102

Smith, Isaac H., 41

Smith, Ruth, 80

Society of Friends. *See* Quakers

Spears, James, 57; brigade drilled by, 44, 45; dismissal of, 83; Fifth Tennessee marched hard by, 51–52; Jewish peddlers and, 35; praise from, 41; speech to soldiers by, 16; Third Tennessee Infantry regiment first mentioned in official records by, 13; as Third Tennessee Infantry regiment brigade commander, 14–15, 38, 41

Sphel, Lt., 21, 97

Spring Hill, Tennessee, 100

Steedman, James B., 96

Stephenson, Philip Saingerfield: on battle of Nashville (1864), 95, 96, 98; on the Union army at the battle of Resaca (1864), 71–72, 74

Statham, W. H., 87

Stokes, Col., 47, 50

Stones River, battle of (1863), 38

Summerville, Georgia, 87

Tabler, Ephram, 90

Tate, John, 41, 51

Taylorsville, Kentucky, 28, 31

Tennessee: political situation on outset of the Civil War of, 1, 3. *See also specific towns*

Terrill, William R., 29

Third Tennessee Infantry regiment: first mention in official records of, 13; mustered into service, 12; mustered out of service, 104

Thomas, George, 34, 41; as Army of the Cumberland commander, 69; at battle of Chattanooga (1863), 53; Nashville defended by during Franklin-Nashville Campaign (1864), 91, 94, 97, 98

Thompson, Dave, 78, 79

Thompson, Isaac, 36

Thompson, Lewis, 78, 79, 80

Thornburg, Col., 10

Trewhitt, Daniel C., 16

Troutman, Henry H., 100

Troutman, I. I., 84

Troutman, Jacob A., 84, 102

Troutman, W. S., 46

Tullahoma, Tennessee, 89; cattle herded to, 81–82

Twelfth Illinois Cavalry regiment, 80

Twenty-Fourth Kentucky Infantry regiment, 97

Unionism: in East Tennessee, 1, 16–19; Quakers on, 12

Vermillion (Illinois) Quaker Meeting, 79, 80

Vicksburg, Mississippi: Union capture of (1863), 49

Ward, Jacob, 31

Waynesboro, Tennessee, 102, 103

Webster, William C., 89

West Tennessee: secessionism in, 1

Wide Awakes, 2; uniforms of pictured, 2

Wheeler, Joseph, 81

Williamsburg, Kentucky, 13, 26
Wilson's Creek, battle of (1861), 67

Yates, Ben, 49

Yates, James, 67, 68, 75
Young, Lot D.: on Sherman's army, 70
Young, Martin, 30